Melannie Svoboda, SND

Sunflower Seeds of *hope*

REFLECTIONS & PRAYERS TO NOURISH YOUR FAITH

TWENTY-THIRD PUBLICATIONS
twentythirdpublications.com

There is a seed of hope in every season.
Seek it. Find it. Cradle it in your hands.
Then give all you are and have
to claim it as your own.

MELANNIE SVOBODA, SND

Twenty-Third Publications
977 Hartford Turnpike Unit A
Waterford, CT 06385
(860) 437-3012 or (800) 321-0411
twentythirdpublications.com

Photo credits: cover, stock.adobe.com/Mira Drozdowski; interior, stock.adobe.com/Vitalina Rybakova

ISBN: 978-1-62785-827-4
Printed in the U.S.A.

CONTENTS

Winter

Spring

INTRODUCTION

Since 2012, I have been writing a blog called *Sunflower Seeds: Celebrating Everyday Spirituality*. Each Monday I post a reflection on some aspect of spirituality—the *everyday* kind of spirituality. This includes things like gazing at a sunflower... praying in a rocking chair... filling the bird feeder... volunteering at an animal shelter... puttering in the garden... laughing with friends... slicing a green pepper... wondering about God... singing at Mass... saying goodbye to a loved one...

Many of my blog readers suggested I put some of my reflections into book form. This is that book. It is composed of forty reflections edited from my blog (www.melanniesvobodasnd.org).

Sunflower Seeds of Hope is intended for people who are curious about God, the natural world, daily life, spirituality—and the interplay among them. It's for people who are drawn to prayer as well as those who struggle with prayer. For people whose faith is strong or whose faith needs some shoring up. And for people who are trying to find God in the events and circumstances they see in the world today—and experience in their everyday life.

The book is arranged in four parts: Summer, Fall, Winter, Spring. Seasonal reflections can be found under the respective season. Those dealing with Advent or Christmas, for example, can be found under Winter; for Lent and Easter, under Spring.

The setup of each chapter is simple. After each reflection, there are a few reflection questions for individual pondering or group sharing. Next, I suggest a video (usually a song) from YouTube that echoes the theme of each reflection. On my blog, I invite my readers to comment on the reflection, adding their own insights or personal experiences. I have included a couple of readers' comments for each reflection. And finally, I have included space for you to write your own response to each chapter.

In writing this book, my prayer for all of us is this:

> May we grow in our awareness of God's presence in our everyday lives...

> May we continue to expand the circle of our love and care for others...

> And may our hope be rooted in the love and power of our Divine Creator, our brother Jesus, and our amazing Holy Spirit.

Summer

*Deep summer is when laziness
finds respectability.*
SAM KEEN

*I have only to break into the tightness of
a strawberry, and I see summer.*
TONI MORRISON

If you're not barefoot, you're overdressed.
ANONYMOUS

1. Why Sunflower Seeds?

Why the title *Sunflower Seeds*?

First of all, because sunflowers are just plain beautiful! When I was growing up on our small farm in northeast Ohio, we often grew sunflowers. Even back then, I admired their tall, sturdy stalks. Most of those sunflowers grew to be much taller than I was. Some even towered over my dad, who was 6 foot 4! I also loved the sunflowers' bright yellow petals. They always looked cheerful to me, even on an overcast or rainy day. And finally, I was fascinated by their "faces" composed of scores of rich, dark seeds.

But sunflowers are not only beautiful, they are bountiful. They first appeared in Central and North America. Now they can be found all over the world in areas that are not desert, tropic, or tundra. Russia and Ukraine produce fifty-three percent of the world's sunflower seeds. A typical field of sunflowers produces millions of seeds. When toasted, these seeds can become a tasty snack for humans. Left in the field or harvested, the seeds provide life-saving nourishment for livestock, countless birds, and other animals, such as squirrels and chipmunks, during the long, cold winter. When crushed, sunflower seeds yield a rich oil low in cholesterol (some say it rivals olive oil in quality). And did you know that the cruder oil of sunflowers can be made into soap and candles?

Beauty. Bounty. Rich oil. What more could the sunflower give us? There is one more thing: a powerful symbol—an icon if you will—for our spiritual life. Let me explain.

Tradition tells us that sunflowers always follow the sun: That is, they turn their "faces" in the direction of the sun, no matter where it is in the sky. Science has shown that this is not entirely true. Young sunflowers follow the sun, but mature sunflowers tend to face east to get the morning sun. Warm sunflowers attract more pollinators.

St. Julie Billiart, the foundress of the Sisters of Notre Dame, liked sunflowers. As a little girl growing up in southern France, she often saw large fields of sunflowers spread across the rolling hills around her. Julie thought of this natural movement of the young sunflower as an ideal for the spiritual life. Like the sunflower, she said, we should "turn always toward God," who is our sun and our source of life and nourishment.

Sunflower Seeds seems an appropriate title for a book on everyday spirituality. For, as I see it, the ever-present challenge of the spiritual life is this: to keep facing and moving in the right direction. Which direction? Toward our Creator God, who beckons us with open arms; toward Jesus, who not only leads us along the way but *is* the way; and toward the Spirit, who lavishes upon us God's own strength and grace for our earthly journey.

If I could, I would now present each one of you with an actual sunflower. But since that's not possible, I'm giving you a virtual one in the form of this little prayer:

May the reflections in this book
encourage all of us to grow tall and strong in our faith,
to be generous with our "seeds" that will help nourish others,
and to journey through our daily life
always following the sun!

FOR REFLECTION

Did anything stand out for you in this reflection?
Any words, phrases, or ideas?

Did you learn anything new about sunflowers?

Can you think of anything else in nature that has helped you in living your spiritual life?

YouTube Video ≪≪≫ "Sunflower Growing from Seed to Flower" (100 Days Time-lapse)

Readers' Comments ≪≪≫

"I had no idea that sunflowers had so many uses, so much potential."

"Sunflowers found me. I became obsessed with them during a very trying time in my late twenties. I began decorating my apartment with sunflowers. I now refer to myself as one of 'the Son's Flowers.'"

My Reflections ≪≪≫

 ## 2. Porches

I like porches. I did a little research and reflection on porches and here's what I came up with. First, a definition. A porch is a covered shelter projecting from a building. Often it is not enclosed except for a railing—although some porches have latticework, screens, or even windows.

Researchers say the front porch has great cultural and historic significance. It connected people to nature, fostering their appreciation for the outdoors. The porch became an outdoor living room where the family often gathered.

In addition, the porch was a link between the private and public life of people. In cities, people often spoke to other families from their front porches or greeted their neighbors as they walked down the street. The porch helped to foster a sense of community.

But the front porch began to disappear in the 1950s. Its demise is attributed to three major factors: the car, air conditioning, and television. The increase in car traffic produced noise and exhaust fumes that drove people from their front porches and into their backyards. Cars also enabled families to go places instead of staying home and sitting on their porches. In addition, air conditioning chased people from their hot porches to the cool interior of their homes. And finally, TV lured people inside to watch their favorite shows.

As I walk or drive around the older part of my town, Chardon, I see many old Victorian houses with huge porches. Some porches wrap around the house on three sides. But smaller and newer homes, built after the 1940s, seem to have small front porches or no porches at all. I notice, however, that many of these homes have decks or patios in the backyard. Some newer homes have large front porches, but I seldom see anyone sitting on them.

Growing up, I lived in a big yellow farmhouse built around 1890. Our house originally had a wraparound porch. But when my parents bought the house in 1942, they had two thirds of the porch removed. Still, the house retained three porches: a front porch off the living room, a side porch off the dining room, and a small enclosed back porch off the kitchen. In the summer, my parents often sat on the front porch after supper. We kids sometimes joined them, plopping down on the porch steps. It was a relaxing place to be. (The night before I left for the convent, I sat on that front porch with my parents for the last time. I cherish that memory.)

In her book *Ordinary Places, Sacred Spaces*, Evelyn Mattern devotes a chapter to porches. She says that front porches are significant for another reason than the ones I've mentioned. "Porches nurture self-expression," she writes. "Those who can't afford fancy flowerpots, elegant trellises, and outdoor furniture find that painted kitchen chairs and ancient rockers do very well. Some of the poorest neighborhoods in the North and South have some of the prettiest, most flower-decked and vine-covered porches. They are places in the sun, places in the shadows, where we can dream what seems impossible indoors."

For Reflection

What has been your experience of porches?

Do you regret the demise of front porches?

Do we have anything today that can foster what porches used to foster: love for nature, family togetherness, a sense of community, or self-expression?

YouTube Video

"If the World Had a Front Porch," by Tracy Lawrence (official video or video with lyrics)

Readers' Comments

"We had a huge porch that faced the St. Clair River in Michigan. We were on that porch from early spring to the end of fall. All our family members were invited to come. It was like an open house party all year long."

"Memories from the big porch of our summer home in Brank Rock, Massachusetts: laughter, fun, sweet corn, big tomatoes, birthday celebrations, and listening to every Red Sox game on a crackling radio. Being outside on the porch made us more aware of the blessings that surrounded us—birds, flowers, and one another."

3. Prayer: Sniffing and Sifting for the Kingdom

I was thinking about prayer recently. (I confess: It's often easier *to think about* prayer than it is to pray!) I came up with two metaphors for prayer that I like: sniffing and sifting. Neither is original to me. Both metaphors are based on the fact that Jesus said the kingdom of God is in our midst, but its presence is not always obvious. Similarly, God's action in our lives is not always readily perceivable. So, we must *sniff out* the kingdom. And we must *sift through* the stuff of daily life to find God—or (as the title of one of my books puts it), we must *rummage for God* in all the nooks and crannies of our lives.

Many years ago, I heard a talk by a priest in a large auditorium. He said, "We must all develop *kingdom noses.*" This means we must go through life *sniffing* for God's kingdom in our midst. To demonstrate what he meant, he walked back and forth across the stage with his nose up in the air, sniffing. He was a tall man, so seeing him sniffing like that was quite a sight. Though we may not actually *see* the kingdom, he said, we may occasionally *catch its scent*—and that scent alone can sustain and direct us.

Here's an example. Think of times when you detected the aroma of something you love. Perhaps, as a child, you came into the house after school and smelled chocolate chip cookies baking. You didn't see the cookies, but the aroma was enough to bring a wide smile to your face. You might have thought you had to be good to be worthy of those cookies, so the aroma alone may have influenced your behavior. And one sniff of those cookies was a kind of promise, too—a promise of "perfect joy" in the future! Similarly, good prayer can bring us the deep knowledge that we are loved. It can influence our decisions and choices. It can remind us of God's promises and bring us joy.

Prayer also makes us more attentive to the aromas of goodness all around us: compassion, gentleness, courage, joy, beauty, loving relationships, heroic generosity. In addition, prayer can help us notice what "stinks" in life: greed, hatred, dishonesty, war, poverty, violence. But good prayer helps us take actions that can lessen or even eradicate life's bad odors.

Another metaphor for prayer is sifting. One image of sifting comes to me from the old westerns I used to watch on TV. Sometimes the prospectors sifted for gold in the earth. They'd put some dirt onto a screen, pour water on it, and shake it back and forth. The small pieces of dirt went through the screen, leaving behind large clumps and pebbles. But sometimes what was left behind was a bright gold nugget! Prayer is like that. It helps us to sift through our everyday to find the gold nuggets of life: genuinely good people, a line from Scripture that speaks to our very soul, the incredible beauty of a particular flower or song.

Today, let us pray for "kingdom noses." May we sniff the air we live in with the hope of detecting a "heavenly scent." And let us pray for patience as we sift through all the "stuff" of our daily life in search of those precious gold nuggets of Divinity.

FOR REFLECTION

Did either of these metaphors speak to you and your experience with prayer? If so, how?

What other metaphors for prayer do you like?

Jesus was a master of metaphor. Which metaphors of his are you drawn to and why?

YouTube Video "Holy as a Day Is Spent," by Carrie Newcomer

Readers' Comments

"I like the idea of the 'kingdom nose' and sniffing around for God. What a perfect metaphor! An aroma is not visible or audible... Keep on sniffing!"

"The song really moved me today. There are so many ways that God sends his love to us if only we look at our day with the eyes of our heart and soul."

My Reflections

4. Why Is There So Much Good in the World?

Does the title of this reflection surprise you? Did you think the word *good* was a mistake? It's not. Years ago, I read something in M. Scott Peck's book *The Road Less Traveled*. He said that throughout his long career as a practicing psychologist, he often heard his clients ask, "Why is there so much evil in the world?" But not one person ever asked him, "Why is there so much GOOD in the world?"

His experience raises a question: Why are we more apt to dwell on what's wrong in the world and in our personal life, rather than on what's right? Why do the news media focus on evil rather than good, on vice rather than virtue, on corruption rather than honesty? One reason they do, of course, is to call our attention to what needs fixing in our society. That's one of their main jobs. Another reason might be because we humans tend to find evil intriguing.

But shouldn't we find goodness fascinating? Instead of wondering why so many people are crabby, shouldn't we be amazed that so many people are pleasant? Instead of noticing how rude some individuals are, shouldn't we be in awe of the kindness we encounter every day—people smiling, opening doors for one another, speaking respectfully, giving others a break in traffic, offering their time and money for those in need?

We must not deny or ignore what's wrong in the world. At the same time, we cannot let what's wrong deter us from doing good. Rather, on a regular basis, we must notice and appreciate the goodness and beauty we see every day. Perhaps during prayer, we can start a list: "What's right with my life right now?" or "What's good in our world?" or "What things am I grateful for today?" We might want to share our list with others.

History can give us a valuable perspective on the present. Here are a few pieces of good news based on a historic perspective:

In the past five decades, the global adult literacy rate rose from 67% to 87%: males 90% and females 82.7%. For centuries, slavery was a common global practice. From its founding in 1776, for example, the United States not only allowed slavery, it had laws to protect the institution of slavery. Today, slavery is outlawed in most countries in the world. Today, nearly 80% of countries have laws protecting children from violence. In 1962 there were 9,214 protected nature reserves in the world; today, there are 295,574.

Citing examples of good news must not lead to complacency. Though slavery is illegal in most countries, it continues to exist in many parts of the world—in a variety of different forms. Though most countries have laws protecting children, those laws are not always enforced. So, too, we may have increased the number of protected nature reserves worldwide, but we are dealing with a global environmental crisis that can have devastating consequences for the entire planet.

As Christians, we base our lives on the everlasting Good News of the gospel and on God's unfailing love for us. During this time of so much bad news, let us not forget in whom our faith resides. So, this week, take time to notice and pray about the good you see in our world. And, more importantly, make a contribution, by your presence and deeds, to the good things already happening in our world.

FOR REFLECTION

What good news have you noticed lately in your life and in the world?

What helps you to cope with bad news?

YouTube Video ⟶ "For the Beauty of the Earth" (John Rutter version with lyrics)

Readers' Comments ⟶

"Today's song took me back to Buseesa, Uganda, where I ministered. Every evening, I would venture out into the inner courtyard and sit on the steps in the garden. Caesar, our watchdog, would come and lay his big black head on my lap, and we would admire God's glorious painting of the Milky Way. Then I would burst into my rendition of 'For the Beauty of the Earth.'"

"As for ways to cope with bad news, Jesus set the example for us: prayer, solitude, treasuring children, love of nature, seeing people's hearts, proactive deeds, a 'can do' attitude, Scripture."

My Reflections ⟶

5. A Cheer for Grandmother Orcas!

Today let's talk about grandmother orcas, those sleek black-and-white whales that are so beautiful. But before I get to the grandmother part, let me say a few words about the orca part. We *Homo sapiens* have given these majestic creatures a terrible name. *Orca* comes from *orcinus*, a word meaning "from hell." We also dub these creatures "killer whales." How did they get such terrible names?

One reason is due to their huge size. Adult males average thirty feet in length, while females are about twenty feet. Because they are so big, orcas require five hundred pounds of food (fish, seals, sea lions, and even other whales) each day to survive. Unfortunately, their simple need for lots of food can look like rapacity or malice. Hence, we humans call them "killers," a word that unjustly implies criminal intent. But orcas are no more killers than the robin hunting for worms or you, eating a cheeseburger for lunch!

Now let's talk about grandmother orcas. Female orcas share a trait with female *Homo sapiens* that is rare among mammals: They go through menopause. This means they stop reproducing in their forties—yet they can live for another forty or more years. To appreciate what they do with the rest of their lives, we must remember that orcas live in family groups called pods. The older females stay in their pod and are literally the grandmothers to many of the younger orcas. It's different with the males. Male orcas in one pod mate with females in another pod. After their liaison, they return home to their original pod—until the next mating season. One consequence of this behavior is that orca calves don't know their fathers or grandfathers. (What a pity!)

But young orcas do know their grandmothers. These females boost the survival rate of orca calves and the entire pod. Because they have more years of experience than their daughters, they know where to find salmon when food is scarce. These grandmas also care for the calves while their mothers leave the pod and hunt for fish. Orcas communicate with each other. Each pod has a unique dialect. Grandmothers help teach the young orcas the dialect of their pod.

Scientists have collected forty years of data on the survival of 378 orca calves off the coasts of Washington and British Columbia.

They found that offspring whose grandmothers had recently died had a mortality rate 4.5 times higher than those with living grandmothers! Scientists also found that adult male orcas whose mother dies have a higher rate of mortality too. Orcas, like humans, seem to be deeply affected by the death of their kin.

What does all of this have to do with us? It can make us appreciate the role of grandparents in our own lives. Grandparents are often wisdom figures for their grandchildren. They pass on valuable experience to the next generations. They regularly share information about their particular human "pod" or family. In addition, grandparents often help care for their grandchildren while parents are out seeking a living. Grandparents expand the circle of love surrounding their grandchildren. Their very presence says, "Yes, Mommy and Daddy love you—but so do Grandma and Grandpa!" That's a lot of love!

FOR REFLECTION

What did you learn from your grandparents?

If your grandparents are deceased, do you have any questions you regret not asking them when they were alive?

If you are a grandparent, what's the best part of being one?

YOUTUBE VIDEO
"Grandmother Song (Canal Dany Matos)," sung by Sheffy Oren Bach

READERS' COMMENTS

"Growing up, I had just one grandmother, Grandma Theresa M., as she signed everything. We were lucky enough to live with her and to learn to love as she loved—God, family, Church."

"It's a great joy to be a grandparent of four beautiful grandchildren and, in effect, to get a second chance at parenting. There's so much one learns about parenting the first time around. But your own children grow up so fast, there's little time to reflect on lessons learned and how to improve. That is, until God blesses you with grandchildren."

MY REFLECTIONS

6. Morning Rituals

Do you have any morning rituals? Do you grab a cup of coffee or tea, check your email, sit quietly for a few moments, or talk to God?

In his book *Earth Works*, Scott Russell Sanders describes one of his morning rituals. In the chapter entitled "A Private History of Awe," he says he always begins his day with some form of meditation. He writes: "When I rise from meditation each morning, I gaze through an uncurtained window at the waking world, and I bow." He draws his hands together to his chest, palms pressed together, and bends slightly from the waist. "The gesture is plain enough," he says, "but its meaning is elusive."

Since moving into this apartment in Notre Dame Village (which is attached to our provincial center), I have incorporated a new ritual into my morning. While still in my pajamas, and before getting my coffee, I step out onto my second-floor balcony. (I prefer to call it my porch.) I do this every day at about 5 a.m. no matter what the weather is doing outside. Usually, I don't see any other human beings. As I stand there, I feel utterly alone.

If you were to ask me why I do this ritual every morning, I could give you several answers. First, I'm inquisitive. I want to know what kind of a day I am awakening to. What's the temperature? Any precipitation, wind, clouds? Yet, my reasons go beyond mere meteorological curiosity. I just love to be outdoors. But since my work keeps me indoors a lot, I have to make a conscious effort to get outside. This little ritual assures that I get outside every single day.

Perhaps the main reason I stand on my porch every morning before dawn is because I love reveling in God's handiwork: the setting moon, the twinkling stars, the swaying trees, the fresh air, the silence. I often talk to these natural entities. I compliment the moon, I praise the stars, I breathe in the fresh air. One morning, the moon was so big, so white, so bright, I wanted to shout to my sleeping neighbors, "Hey, everybody! Wake up! Get out here! You've gotta see this moon!" But, of course, I didn't. Instead, I thanked God for another day, stepped inside, grabbed my coffee, and began my "formal" prayer.

Toward the end of Sanders' chapter on awe, he explains more clearly why he bows to his uncurtained window every morning. He describes how the natural world fills him with wonder and awe. Then he says, "I am not saying that nature is God, for at this time in my life, with my children grown and my beard turning white, I have given up all opinions about God. I am saying that what we call nature, this all-embracing power and pattern, fills me with joy and inspires me with profound respect for all that lives. I am saying that mountains and mosquitoes, rivers and rhododendrons, you and I are utterances of this power. I am saying that this persuasive, unnamable, shaping energy, glimpsed in the whorl of skin on a thumb or the spiral of stars in a distant nebula, is what compels me to bow at a brightening window each morning."

And I would say that my few minutes outside on my porch each morning centers me. It connects me to the greater pulsating world of which I am a teeny-weeny participant. It leads me to say with deep joy, "Thank you, my dear, sweet God—for everything!"

FOR REFLECTION

Do you have any morning rituals? If so, what are they? Why do you do them?

In which situations or circumstances do you sense your connectedness with all things?

Does gratitude for the gift of existence ever well up in your heart? If so, when?

YOUTUBE VIDEO "Morning Has Broken," by Cat Stevens

READERS' COMMENTS

"I love your intentionality about going outside every day. I find this inspiring, to continue to embrace what feeds us as our seasons of life and surroundings change."

"I like Edith Stein's quote: 'All I need is a quiet corner where I can talk to God each day as if there were nothing else to do. I try to make myself a tool for God.'"

MY REFLECTIONS

7. Fire Engines: Symbols of Unselfish Loving

I like fire engines. For many reasons. First, I like their bright colors. Most fire engines are red, but many are other colors, such as yellow, lime, orange, blue, white, and even purple. Whatever color, fire engines are bright.

I also like fire engines because they are big. Park a car or even a pickup truck next to one and it is dwarfed. Fire trucks must be big because they carry not only a team of firefighters to a fire, but also heavy equipment such as ladders, fire extinguishers, axes, floodlights, hoses, fire-fighting apparel, and self-contained breathing apparatuses (SCBA). In addition, some fire trucks have on-board water reservoirs.

I like fire engines because they shine and sparkle and make a lot of noise. Their flashing lights and horns warn you that they are coming—usually quite fast. Their sirens can make a variety of sounds, from the traditional wail to the loud "yelp." Most European fire engines use that distinctive "hi-lo" siren.

But the main reason I like fire engines is this: They are beautiful symbols of unselfish love. They represent humanity at its best. As writer Kurt Vonnegut said many years ago, "I can think of no more stirring symbol of man's humanity to man than a fire truck."

Firefighters devote their lives to helping other people—often total strangers. When a call comes, they drop everything and race to the emergency—whether it is a house fire, a bomb explosion, a skyscraper ablaze, a chemical spill, or a forest in flames. Once at the scene, they go about their work with consummate energy and skill. They never stop first and ask the people they are about to help, "What will you give me if I help you?" Or "What is your religious faith?" Or "Whom did you vote for in the last election?" No, firefighters just help—no questions asked.

Firefighters also remind all of us just how precious human life is. They do this by putting themselves in harm's way in an effort to protect and save lives. When they get a call about a horrible situation, they don't say, "Chances are there aren't any survivors, so we don't have to rush." No, because no matter how hopeless the situation might look, they give the benefit of the doubt to life and race to the scene. So long as life *might be there*, they go into action to preserve it. This attitude speaks volumes to me about the sanctity of every human life.

I have been told by people who were raised in the city and attended Catholic schools that as schoolchildren, every time a fire truck went by, the nuns or lay teachers taught them to make the sign of the cross and pray for the firefighters and the people they were going to help. That's a wonderful practice to continue into adulthood.

For me, the real heroes in life are those individuals who give of themselves to others in dramatic and in ordinary ways. That includes firefighters, rescue workers, police officers, military personnel, as well as parents, teachers, and anyone else serving humanity. I'll close with one of my favorite quotes about heroes, by Bob Riley: "Hard times don't create heroes. It is during hard times that the hero within us is revealed."

For Reflection

Do you have any experience with fire engines or firefighters?

Do you have any favorite heroes?

What other symbols of unselfish love do you see in our world today?

YouTube Video "We Are Made for Service," by Sr. Flor (sung by the Dameans)

"I vividly remember my mother making the sign of the cross whenever she heard a siren. I never realized she wasn't the only one who did this! She taught me to pray for those who might be in the fire or in great danger."

"I have two brothers who are police officers. I guess you could say many of the same things about them."

MY REFLECTIONS

8. What the Church Can Learn from AA

Some of my friends belong to Alcoholics Anonymous. They include priests, nuns, and lay people. My admiration for them leads me to conclude that the Church could learn a lot from AA.

First, a little background. Alcoholics Anonymous is a worldwide organization for individuals who have a problem with alcohol. It was founded in 1935 by Bill Wilson and Dr. Bob Smith in Akron, Ohio. Wilson and Smith learned that people could get sober basically by coming together regularly, by believing in each other, and by recognizing the strength of the group. AA has a simple statement of purpose for its members: "To stay sober and help other alcoholics achieve sobriety." Over time, Wilson and Smith devised a Twelve Step Program that transcends gender, age, culture, and religious beliefs. Currently, the worldwide membership in AA is over two million. Members of AA in North America have achieved sobriety for an average of ten years.

What could the Church learn from AA? Let's begin with some words from Frederick Buechner, a minister and author of the memoir *Telling Secrets*. He says: "I believe that what goes on [at AA meetings] is far closer to what Christ meant his Church to be, and what it originally was." He points out that AA has no buildings, no official leadership, and no money. It also has no preachers, no choirs, no fundraising, no advertising, no proselytizing. Buechner says, "They make you wonder if the best thing that could happen to many a church might not be to have its building burn down and to lose all its money." If this happened, says Buechner, "Then all that the people would have left is God and each other."

God and each other. That phrase lies at the heart of what AA is. Maybe the Church needs to remember that the essence of our faith is not our buildings, creeds, or hierarchy. It is God and each other. I am not saying we should get rid of our churches, our creeds, or our leadership. But I am saying we must remember that these components of our faith are secondary, not primary. Someone described AA as a "fellowship of mutual aid." That also seems like a good definition of "church" to me.

Why is AA so effective? It brings people together who *share a common pain*: the pain of addiction. Or, as one friend told me, "AA is for people who have been to hell—or at least to the rim of hell." AA demonstrates that our pain and sorrow have the potential to unite us as nothing else can—not even our joy.

At AA meetings, nobody preaches to anyone. They simply tell their own stories—where they went wrong and how they are trying to get better day by day. Sometimes, one of them takes special responsibility for another member by being available 24/7 if the need arises. There's not much more to AA than that. Yet, healing occurs and miracles happen. So effective has AA been that it has many spin-offs, such as Al-Anon, Overeaters Anonymous, and Gamblers Anonymous. AA has its critics, of course. Some claim it is a cult, yet AA lacks a chief characteristic of most cults: It does not force its members to stay.

AA meetings often end with "The Serenity Prayer," written by American theologian Reinhold Niebuhr in the 1930s. It seems only fitting to conclude this reflection with that prayer:

> *God, grant me the serenity*
> *to accept the things I cannot change,*
> *the courage to change the things I can,*
> *and the wisdom to know the difference.*

FOR REFLECTION

Do you have any experience with AA?

What else could the Church learn from AA?

YOUTUBE VIDEO "The Serenity Prayer Song" (Official Video)

READERS' COMMENTS

"AA is always welcoming. Everything in AA is SUGGESTED. And almost everything I hear on a retreat or read in a spiritual book, I have already heard in AA."

"Scripture, the writings of the saints, AA literature, and other blessed resources demonstrate the pillars of surrender, trust, and wisdom.

Ultimately, Christ invites us all, whether we sit in a basement on folding chairs, in cathedrals, or around our small kitchen tables."

MY REFLECTIONS

9. Everyday Mysticism and a Green Pepper

Sometimes we think mystics were individuals who had extraordinary religious experiences: hearing God's voice, seeing angels, and levitating three feet above the ground. Surely, we think, in modern times most mystics would be medicated. Doctor to mystic: "I notice you're floating three feet above the ground. We have a pill for that."

But the noted twentieth-century Jesuit theologian Karl Rahner wrote, "In the days ahead, you will either be a mystic or nothing at all." For Rahner, mysticism was something available to everyone, because the Divine is accessible to all. Mysticism, then, is not restricted to desert caves or monastery cells. It can be found in office cubicles and kitchens.

What is mysticism? I like this definition by Kaya Oakes: Mysticism is "a transcendent experience of an encounter with God." A mystical experience could happen while taking out the garbage, walking the dog, or having a conversation with a friend. Mysticism is not confined to Christianity: It also runs deep in the Jewish, Buddhist, and Muslim traditions.

For me, mysticism is *seeing something as it really is*. Often coupled with this seeing is the realization of *our connectedness with all that is*. A mystical experience also bestows a sense of profound appreciation for the inherent mystery, goodness, and beauty of which we are a part. Paradoxically, the Divine is often sensed as both very near and very far beyond us.

That brings me to green peppers. I sometimes make my mother's recipe for ground meat, tomato sauce, and elbow macaroni. She called it "Mess," and I feel connected to my mother every time I make it. I also get excited because the recipe calls for one green bell pepper. I love visiting the pepper bin in the produce department. As I approach the bin, I take a moment to gaze upon the peppers, admiring their deep green color, their shiny surface, their gentle, inviting curves. I can almost hear the peppers' tiny voices crying out to me, "Pick me! Pick me! Take me home with you!" I begin my selection by handling each pepper reverently, seeking the perfect size, firmness, and color. Finally, I select "my" pepper. My Chosen Pepper!

When I start to make Mess, I rinse the pepper in cold water. Then, on the cutting board, with a sharp knife, I halve it. As the two pieces fall onto the board, I sniff its familiar earthy aroma. Then I take a moment to gaze at the tiny ecru-colored seeds nestled in the hollow chamber. There are zillions of them! I exaggerate, I know, but I find it hard to curb my excitement!

I wonder: Why are the seeds ecru—and not brown or black, like so many other seeds? I pick up a single seed and admire it. Just think, I muse, inside this tiny seed is a future *pepper plant*! Each seed bears the genetic code to reproduce itself—that is, to extend itself into the future. Now, who came up with that idea? Was the Divine Creator so enthralled with the sight and taste of the first pepper that she planted this ingenious power inside peppers (and everything else of value) to live on into the future?

I dice my pepper and sauté it in a little oil. When it's soft, I spoon the pieces out. Then I cut up a medium onion and sauté that too. (Have I mentioned how excited I get over onions? Don't get me started...)

I will eventually dine on this cherished family recipe. And here's the best part: That beautiful chosen pepper will become part of me! How cool is that?

Some people think a mystical experience has to be extraordinary. But I believe many of us are "mystics of the everyday."

FOR REFLECTION

What takes my breath away?

What makes me sense my connectedness to the cosmos?

What makes me feel the nearness and beyondness of God?

YOUTUBE VIDEO "Love," by George Herbert (1593–1633) – performing poetry

READERS' COMMENTS

"I have always loved that poem by George Herbert. As I listened to the song, I was reminded of a prayer said after communion in the Byzantine tradition: 'Behold, what has touched your lips, shall take away your iniquities, shall cleanse you of all your sins.'"

"Thank you for making such a profound subject so real and accessible in such a reverent way."

10. The Hands of Jesus

> Simon's mother-in-law lay sick with a fever. They imme-
> diately told [Jesus] about her. He approached, grasped
> her hand, and helped her up. Then the fever left her and
> she waited on them. MARK 1:30-31

He grasped her hand. How did it feel to have her hand grasped by the hand of Jesus? Did she sense the strength in his hand? Did she feel any calluses? Did she sense tenderness in his touch? After reading this story, I wondered: How many times are Jesus' hands mentioned in the gospels? And what are they doing?

Jesus' hands brought healing. One day a leper says to him, "If you wish, you can make me clean." And Jesus stretches out his hand, saying, "I will do it. Be made clean," and immediately the leper was cured (Matthew 8:2–3). Jesus restores sight to the blind man. He takes the man by the hand and leads him outside the village. Imagine walking hand in hand with Jesus! Then he puts spittle on the man's eyes. When the man says he sees only vaguely, Jesus repeats the gesture and the man's sight is restored (Mark 8:23–25).

Jesus cures the deaf man in a similar way, putting his fingers in the man's ears and even touching his tongue (Mark 7:31–35).

Jesus' hands brought people back to life. When he meets Jairus's twelve-year-old daughter, she is already dead. But he takes her by the hand, and she rises (Matthew 9:25–26). When he encounters the widow in Nain burying her only son, he stops the funeral procession, touches the bier, and tells the young man to arise. The widow's son sits up and begins to speak (Luke 7:11–17).

Throughout the gospels, Jesus' hands are doing all kinds of other things too. They bless and play with children. When the adulteress is brought before him, Jesus' hand writes something mysterious in the sand. His hands help distribute bread to feed the hungry crowds. They wield a whip to drive the money changers out of the temple.

At the Last Supper, his hands wash the feet of his disciples and dry them with a towel. His hands break the bread and distribute it to his disciples. In Gethsemane, Jesus' hands are clenched in agony as he begs the Father, "Let this cup pass from me... but not my will but yours be done." His hands are bound by the Roman soldiers as he is led away. And finally, before he is lifted up on the cross, Jesus' hands are pierced with nails.

Even after his resurrection, Jesus' hands are busy. When he first appears to his stunned disciples, his hands bless them with peace. A week later, Jesus invites Thomas to touch the wounds in his hands to convince Thomas that he is really Jesus. Another time, he serves his apostles a barbecued breakfast on a beach, a breakfast made with his own hands.

St. Teresa of Avila, that great sixteenth-century mystic, shared these famous words: "Christ has no body now but yours... no hands, no feet, no eyes, no voice but yours." Pay attention to your hands this week. Spend a few minutes just gazing at them and thanking God for the incredible gift they are. Then notice the hands of others. Watch little children just learning to use their hands. Observe the hands of workers such as cashiers, mechanics, cooks, hair stylists, doctors, the priest at Mass, the elderly.

And finally, reflect on some of the things you do with your hands regularly. How do you use them, in imitation of Jesus, to bring healing, life, and love into the lives of others?

YouTube Video ⟨⟨⟨ "His Hands," by Kenneth Cope – A Tribute to Jesus Christ – Jackman Music

Readers' Comments ⟨⟨⟨

"What struck me the first time I served as a Eucharistic minister was the hands of all the people. They were all different. Some were strong, some small, some large—but they were all reaching out to receive Jesus. It was a powerful experience."

"One of my memories as a child was observing my mother's hands as she worked—but mostly as she prayed. As her hands became much older, they were still beautiful, but instead of her hand holding mine, I was holding hers."

My Reflections ⟨⟨⟨

Fall

*Autumn carries more gold in its pockets
than all the other seasons.*

JIM BISHOP

*The weather just went from 90 to 55
like it just saw a state trooper.*

ANONYMOUS

*Delicious Autumn! My very soul is wedded
to it, and if I were a bird I would fly about
the earth seeking successive autumns!*

GEORGE ELIOT

11. Three Images of Autumn

Although I love all four seasons, I have a special fondness for autumn. Where I live, it comes with cooler temperatures, shorter days, and brilliantly colored foliage. Here are three images of fall for your pondering.

The Golden Woods

As I approach the golden woods, I hear God say to me: "Do come in! I've painted these woods gold and brown and yellow just for you... Step inside and swish your feet among the crisp fallen leaves. I've created that swishing sound just for you too. Look up... look down... look all around. Listen to the silence and the occasional sound of falling leaves or acorns... or a squirrel or chipmunk rustling among the leaves. Breathe in the cool, crisp air. Reach down and pick up a leaf and look at it closely, noticing its color... its veins... its dampness or dryness. This spot in the woods is all for you. All!... Walk around if you wish... or sit on a fallen log... or even kneel on the carpet of leaves if you want... I know, my beloved child, you are busy doing many good and beautiful things for me and for mine, but I hope you make some time to enjoy this special season of the year with me."

A Thank-You Note to God for Apples

Dear God, apples get a bad rap in the Bible. Adam and Eve ate an apple and were cast out of the Garden of Eden. But the story doesn't say the fruit was an apple. Maybe it was a pear, a pomegranate, or even a banana. So, today I thank you for apples—all 7,500 cultivated varieties of them! Thank you for red, green, yellow, orange apples—and for white and rainbow-colored ones too! Thank you for the many uses for apples: cider, juice, applesauce, apple butter, apple pie, apple strudel, apple turnovers, apple fritters, Apple Brown

Betty, and the list goes on. The proverb says, "An apple a day keeps the doctor away." Thank you for their many health benefits: They contain no fat and no cholesterol, are high in fiber and antioxidants, and are said to improve memory and reduce the risk of cancer, obesity, heart disease, and diabetes. But most importantly, thank you, God, for the simple round beauty of apples and their juicy taste, whether sweet or tart or somewhere in between! The day you made the first apple, I say you were having a very good day!

The Burning Bush

The so-called burning bush is a deciduous shrub that is green most of the year. But in autumn, its leaves turn a brilliant red before they fall. I had a friend who turned her small backyard into a verdant garden. I asked her once if she ever considered planting a burning bush in her garden. She said she had thought about it but decided not to. "Fifty weeks of ordinariness for a two-week splurge of riotous color?" she asked. Then she added, "I didn't think it was worth it."

She had a point. At the same time, I wondered: Should we limit our appreciation of this bush only to the brief time it turns red? Or can we appreciate it all year long—when its branches are filled with tiny buds or with lush green leaves—or even when its lack of leaves in winter reveals the delicate but sturdy structure of its bare branches? I pray: God of the ordinary and extraordinary, give me a discerning eye to see the extraordinary even in the ordinary things of daily life. And help me to appreciate the beauty in all the seasons of my life too!

FOR REFLECTION

Did anything catch your attention in this reflection?

What are your thoughts and feelings about autumn?

YOUTUBE VIDEO "Stunning Fall Foliage in New England" by Ally Marie Brown

READERS' COMMENTS

"Burning bushes are resilient. We have a few we've moved several times, or all but chopped down due to overgrowth. But they came back year after year. How often do I feel disrupted by change or cut down by life's challenges? But I look at those shrubs and say, 'If they can do it, I can too.'"

*"Your reflection reminds me of the book **The Fall of Freddie the Leaf** by Leo Buscaglia. I read it to my class every year. The kids just love it!"*

MY REFLECTIONS

12. The Zacchaeus Story

The story of Jesus' encounter with Zacchaeus (Luke 19:1–10) begins with this curious statement: "Jesus intended to pass through the town [Jericho]." So, even Jesus changed his plans sometimes. What made him change his plans here? It is a person. Zacchaeus.

Zacchaeus, a Jew, is a tax collector. That means he is in cahoots with the Romans, the occupying forces. No wonder he is hated by his fellow Jews! And Zacchaeus is not just *any* tax collector. He is a *chief* tax collector. He rose in the ranks. How? By being good at what he did. He collected those taxes for those Romans no matter what. No hard luck story would warm the cockles of his heart. No: You paid what you owed, or else! The Romans must have loved this guy!

(Confession: I'm getting tired of typing Zacchaeus, so from now on I'm going to call him Zack.) Zack *was short in stature*. That genetic happenstance plays into the story. He came to see Jesus, but because he's short, he *can't see Jesus*. And no one in that crowd is going to say to this pariah, "Oh, Zack! Come and stand here in front of me so you can see Jesus!" No. So, quick-thinking Zack scrambles up a nearby *sycamore tree*. By pointing out what kind of tree it was, Luke "roots" this story in reality. This story happened in a real place (Jericho), with real people (Jesus and Zack), and with a real tree (a sycamore). (Question: When *you* are "up a tree," do you seek out Jesus? What about when you're *not* up a tree?)

As Jesus passes, he spots Zack in that tree. I bet Jesus smiled when he saw him up there. Then Jesus says, "Zacchaeus, come down quickly, for today I must stay at your house." Jesus calls him by name. How did he know who he was? Probably the same way we all know people in our midst who are not welcome in our circles. Zack's bad reputation preceded him.

But Jesus tells Zack to "come down quickly." He's saying, "Come down, Zack. I'd like to meet you eye-to-eye." (Does Jesus say similar words to us?) Then Jesus adds, "For today I must stay at your house." Wow! The word "must" suggests urgency. And talk about being forward! Jesus invites himself into Zack's house—that is, into *his life*. (Is Jesus doing the same for us?)

Zack scurries down that tree and proudly leads Jesus to his house. I picture the crowd stepping aside so this "odd couple" can pass. I hear them grumbling: "He has gone to stay at the house of a sinner. Tsk! Tsk!" I bet Jesus lost many followers that day.

Next, there's a glaring omission in this story: What did Jesus and Zack talk about during their meal together? I want to know what Jesus said or did that changed Zack from a cold-hearted, conniving, selfish tax collector into a kind-hearted, generous, sorry-for-my-sins, I'll-make-things-right-again kind of guy. But I think I know the answer. It was Jesus. It was Jesus being Jesus.

There's one more thing that touches me in this story. At the end, Jesus says: The "Son of Man [that's Jesus] has come to seek and to save what was lost." It's that little word "seek." Yes, we seek God, we seek Jesus. But our seeking pales in comparison to the Divine seeking that God does for each one of us. In that truth lies our salvation!

We might want to ask ourselves: Who are *we* in this story? Are we Zacchaeus—someone cold-hearted or shunned by others? Or someone profoundly curious about Jesus? Or maybe we're in the crowd, judging others as no good, lost, unworthy of our care. Or (hopefully, at times!) we're Jesus—someone willing to change our plans because someone needs our attention and love.

FOR REFLECTION

What stands out for you in the story of Zacchaeus?

Who are you in the story?

Readers' Comments

"My biggest take away was Jesus' willingness to cross 'political lines,' so to speak, to reach out, to listen to another, not to condemn. That's how hearts are changed."

"Wonderful and inspiring! I admit I am not the brightest or the most dedicated, but I am a seeker like Zack."

My Reflections

13. The Mass as Thanksgiving

Deborah Meister, a writer and artist in St. Louis, Missouri, tells this true story. She was in the church parking lot before Mass one Sunday and overheard a child arguing with his parents. "But I don't want to go to church," he cried. "It's boring!" She thought the father would drag his son kicking and screaming into the church. But instead, the father said to the boy, "I'm going into church to say thank you to God, because God has given us so many wonderful things that aren't boring." And he began to list some of them. The boy listened intently. Soon he began to smile, took his father's hand, and walked into the church.

That father was a theologian without realizing it, for he captured the essence of the Third Commandment in words his little son could understand. We Christians "keep holy the Lord's Day" by gathering in our faith community to give thanks to God for all the blessings we have received. For Catholics, keeping holy the Lord's Day means celebrating Mass as a faith community.

A corollary to our thanks at Mass is this: We take time to relax and enjoy the company of family and friends—whether that means staying longer at the dinner table, watching a movie together, playing games, going for a walk, visiting an elderly relative, or sitting around a fire pit in the evening.

If you ask Catholics why they go to Mass every Sunday, you will probably get a wide range of answers: "I go because I have to... I go to show my love for Jesus... I go to get strength to deal with my problems and worries... I go to be in the company of other believers... I go to be inspired by the prayers, Scriptures, homily, and music." We celebrate Mass for many reasons, but a central reason is to give thanks to God for all our blessings. In fact, the very word *Eucharist* in Greek means *Thanksgiving*.

Do we ever take time on Sunday to name a few blessings of the past week that we are grateful for? We can do this while waiting for Mass to begin, or driving home, or finding a quiet moment later in the day. Our prayer can be simple. Here are a few questions to answer. Our answers will form our own Sunday litany of thanksgiving.

Who encouraged you this past week?... Who was kind or thoughtful?... Who surprised you in a good way?... Who helped you in any way? Who made you smile or laugh?... How were you able to help someone?... Where did you see Jesus?... What were some of your challenges this past week?... What were your little accomplishments?... Did anything in creation give you delight, beauty, or peace?... Who inspired you?... Of all the blessings you experienced this past week, which one are you most grateful for?

At the end of Mass, the priest says, "Go in peace." That word "go" means much more than "You can leave now." It also means "Go and spread the Good News of the gospel!" or "Go and be Jesus for others!" or "Go in peace, knowing that God is with you wherever you go this coming week!"

For Reflection

If you go to Mass, why do you go? If you do not go to Mass, why don't you go?

What are you most grateful for this past week (or this Thanksgiving)?

YouTube Video
"Thanks Be to God," by Stephen Dean (sung by the SSP Choir) or "Thanksgiving Song," by JJ Heller (Official Lyric Video)

Readers' Comments
"Grateful for dearest friends. For my community of faith at church. For five years of sobriety. And grateful for the month of November, which has its own austere splendor."

"In my senior years, my thanks have been for all the things I used to take for granted: a roof, potable water, the peaceful community I call home. All of it is gift. I'm aware of the many others who struggle for the barest necessities—a reminder of the corporal works of mercy."

14. A Kitchen Is a Holy Place

A kitchen is a holy place, as holy as any sanctuary.

What was the kitchen of your childhood like? When I was growing up, we had a bright yellow kitchen. It wasn't very big: just large enough for a stove, a refrigerator, and a sink with counters and cupboards extending on both sides. Two windows perched above the sink, facing east and overlooking our shaded side yard. Our large kitchen table was in the adjoining dining room.

For me, the kitchen was a magical place that churned out all kinds of good stuff: hot oatmeal for a winter breakfast, homemade soups for lunch, and meatloaf and mashed potatoes for supper. On Saturday mornings, tantalizing aromas came from the kitchen: aromas of Bohemian sweet bread (hoska), kolachky, and nut rolls.

As I grew older, my mother shared some of her culinary magic tricks with me, teaching me to make cookies, brownies, and cakes—all from scratch. I eventually graduated to creating simple meals for the family.

I can also remember the kitchens of every convent I ever lived in. Some were huge industrial-sized kitchens that turned out three meals a day for a hundred or more sisters. Others were normal-sized kitchens where sisters took turns cooking for six or so. In the old days we had "cook sisters" who toiled long hours preparing meals, not only for our larger convents but also for boarding schools, college resident halls, and employees. These dedicated sisters got up before the rest of us (and we got up at 5 a.m.!). After supper, they were often canning and freezing fruits and vegetables, sometimes late into the night.

Through it all, these cook sisters usually exuded joy, humor, and wisdom. If I had a problem, I often went to a cook sister to pray for the situation. I somehow felt that her prayers were more efficacious than mine.

In her book *Ordinary Places, Sacred Spaces*, Evelyn Mattern says this about kitchens: "Kitchens are obvious contemplative places. So many rhythmic and repetitive actions keep them humming: peeling potatoes, cutting up and grating vegetables, stirring sauces and soups, kneading bread, making coffee, washing dishes, feeding cats and dogs. These actions offer meditative possibilities, breathing moments in the midst of a hectic day." Her words make me wonder: With today's frenzied pace, have we have lost some of these rhythmic actions so conducive to contemplation?

Kitchens exude intimacy. We tend to share our kitchen with family and close friends. And, as all realtors know, kitchens sell homes.

When Jesus sent his disciples to get a room to celebrate the Passover, he must have known that a nearby kitchen was part of the deal. Da Vinci's famous painting of the Last Supper, as beautiful as it is, did us a disservice. It made us think this event was a quiet, private affair involving thirteen men. I like some of the modern depictions of the Last Supper (by Bohdan Piasecki and Nora Kelly, for example) that include women and children. Mattern writes: "As Jesus and the twelve reclined at the table to share these last, sacred intimacies, the women disciples were preparing food nearby and carrying it to the table."

Yes, a kitchen is a holy place, as holy as any sanctuary.

FOR REFLECTION ⚜

What are your memories of the kitchens of your childhood?

Is your current kitchen a "contemplative space"? Why or why not?

Do you agree or disagree: "Kitchens exude a certain level of intimacy"?

YOUTUBE VIDEO ⚜ "One Bread, One Body," by John Foley

READERS' COMMENTS ⚜

"My grandmother's kitchen was a farmhouse kitchen where not only the bread happened, but discussions, sharing stories, the tending of childhood wounds, etc. I close my eyes and I see my mom working in her kitchen always in a skirt, an apron, and even heels. Different times for certain, but sacred times in the kitchen."

"To paraphrase Monika Hellwig: Many hearts are laid bare, forgiveness offered, and healing takes place over a cup of coffee or tea in a kitchen."

MY REFLECTIONS ⚜

15. Saying Grace: It's Not Just for Meals Anymore

Most of us are familiar with saying grace, the traditional prayer we say before meals: *Bless us, O Lord, and these, thy gifts, which we are about to receive from thy bounty, through Christ our Lord. Amen.* Praying grace before our meals reminds us of the essential giftedness of food. But isn't all of life a gift?

The British writer G.K. Chesterton thought so. That's why he suggested we say grace not only before meals but also before other activities throughout the day. This is a practice I have adopted over the years.

Upon awakening, for example, while still in bed, I make the sign of the cross or I trace a cross on my forehead. Then I say something like, "Good morning, God" or "Jesus, please bless this day" or "Melannie reporting for duty, Lord." That's my grace before starting my day.

Here are some other times during the day when we can "say grace":

+ *While getting dressed.* Many religious congregations had the practice of praying while putting on the various parts of the religious habit—the dress, cape, veil, etc. I'm not saying we should return to that. But we could utter a simple "Bless my body and all it will do for you today, God" or "Thank you for the clothes I am lucky to have."

+ *Before checking the news.* We can pray for all the individuals and situations we will read or hear about in today's news. We can ask God to make us attentive to the stories that touch us most deeply, stories that might be stirring us to action.

+ *Before driving anywhere.* When beginning any trip, we can utter a quick prayer asking God to bless the purpose of our trip and to help us to drive responsibly. As a child, I remember that when our family came home from a trip—perhaps after visiting our grand-parents—as we pulled into our driveway, my mother would say something like this: "And we thank you, Lord, for a safe journey and a wonderful day."

+ *When getting the cart in the grocery store.* We can thank God for the abundance of food we have to choose from. And we can remind ourselves to pick up something for our local food pantry.

+ *Before meeting with family and friends.* We can say, "Thank you, God, for giving me these individuals in my life." We can also ask God to bless our time together.

+ *Before reading a book, watching a movie, or listening to music.* We can thank God for the arts and the enrichment they bring into our lives.

+ *Before starting a project.* Whether we're writing a report, begin-ning a meeting, cooking a meal, raking leaves, or cleaning a bathroom, we can ask God for the attentiveness and strength to do the project well—and to do it with gratitude and joy.

+ *Before relaxing.* Whether we're puttering in our garden, sitting down to watch our favorite team on TV, heading for the golf course, starting a craft project, or cracking open another novel, we can say thank you to God for having this time to engage in an activity that relaxes us and brings us such joy and satisfaction.

+ *Before going for a walk.* We might thank God for the ability to walk and for having a safe place in which to walk. We can also ask that we might be attentive to the people and things we see along the way.

Grace, then, is not just for meals anymore. It's a way of making us more aware of the countless gifts we receive on any given day. And, more importantly, saying grace intentionally connects us with God, the Giver of all gifts.

YOUTUBE VIDEO ⤳ "Thanksgiving Medley," by Courthouse Road Church

READERS' COMMENTS ⤳

"When I am almost home, at a certain stop sign, I always say, 'Thank you, God, for bringing me home safely.'"

"A few years ago, we had a retreat director who taught us what he called the WIT prayer—with him, in him, through him. So, when I begin a new day, I say to God, 'Live this day with me, in me, through me.' It's a good reminder that I am not alone in whatever I do."

MY REFLECTIONS ⤳

16. What Is Christian Social Teaching?

Wrestling with God, a book by Fr. Ronald Rolheiser, OMI, is inspiring and challenging. You could say I found myself *wrestling* with some sections. Chapter 4, for example, is on the gospel mandate to reach out to the poor. Rolheiser begins with a quote by James Forbes: "Nobody gets to heaven without a letter of reference from the poor." My reaction was: Gulp! And then, "Who's going to write *my* reference letter?"

Rolheiser describes how the Law of Moses *legally obligated* the people to give to the poor in their midst. Here are two examples. Every seventh year, all economic debts were canceled. And at all times, landowners were forbidden to reap the corners of their fields, thus leaving these spaces to be gleaned by the poor. In the book of Ruth, Ruth was gleaning in the fields with other poor women when she met the owner of that field, Boaz, and eventually married him! She and Boaz were the direct ancestors of King David—and Jesus himself. Says Rolheiser, "We have much to learn from this society."

He believes we are basically generous and charitable people. But he maintains that social justice goes beyond individual charitable giving—as important as charitable giving is. Rolheiser then summarizes Christian Social Teaching in ten points. I'm going to summarize his summary in six points.

1. All people have equal dignity, equal rights, and equal access to resources and opportunity. "The riches of this world should flow equally and fairly to all."

2. The right to private property and accumulation of wealth is not an absolute one. It must be subordinated to the common good and to the fact that the goods of the earth are intended for all. In the United States, we have the law of "eminent domain," for example, that gives the government the right to buy your property (for a highway or other public work) even if you do not want to sell. At the same time, the government is legally obligated to pay a fair market price for your land.

3. We are obligated morally to come to the aid of those in need.

4. The current situation in the world where some individuals and nations have excess while others lack basic necessities is immoral, against the teachings of Christ, and must be redressed.

5. The earth itself also has inherent rights. (See Pope Francis's encyclical *Laudato Si'*.)
6. Movement toward the poor is a route to both God and spiritual health.

What do you think of these tenets? Some people say they are naïve and idealistic. They demand too much of us. There's no denying that trying to live Jesus' words in Matthew 25 is tough!

Do you see any evidence of the Church, specific organizations, or real individuals practicing these principles of Christian social justice? Is there any evidence that *you* are trying to live them? What about your family, your parish, or your religious congregation?

When I look at our national and global problems, I'm tempted to throw up my hands in despair and say things like: "But I'm only one person... I'm too old for this now... These problems are too complex... I'm overwhelmed by the injustices I see in the world." Instead, we must heed Jesus' challenging words: "What you do to the least, you do to me."

For Reflection ⋘⋙

What are your responses to the questions posed throughout this reflection?

What do you personally try to do to reach out to the poor?

YouTube Video ⋘⋙ "Matthew 25 35 40" (greasbymethodist)

Readers' Comments ⋘⋙

"Yes, I gulped a bit while reading your words."

"When my autistic grandson was four, we were walking on the street when he let go of my hand and ran to a homeless man and threw his

arms around him. The man started to laugh and said, 'That's the first hug I've had in a long time.'"

MY REFLECTIONS

17. The Ways We Say Goodbye

When we part from another person, we ordinarily say "goodbye" in English. The word "goodbye" is a contraction of the phrase "God be with you." If you squish the four words together, you come up with "goodbye."

The French *adieu* and the Spanish *adios* are similar. They are short for *à Dieu vous commant* and *a Dios vos acomiendo*. Both mean "I commend you to God." I think it's rather wonderful that, in these three languages, our parting words to one another are really a short wish or prayer for them.

The German goodbye is different. It's *auf wiedersehen*, which literally means "until we see each other again." I like that too. It implies that this parting is not final. In English we sometimes say, "See ya!" which implies the same thing. I like the old German proverb that says, "Those who live in the Lord never see each other for the last time."

We say other things to each other when we bid goodbye. I often hear and say, "Take care." I like that, too, for it implies that "You are precious to me, so take care of yourself." Sometimes we say, "Have a good day." Some people think this phrase is so overused it has been rendered meaningless. But I, for one, still like the phrase. I think it fosters good feelings between people—even strangers. The phrase also implies that *we*, to a certain extent, determine what kind of a day we're going to have—often by our attitude. (I read somewhere: If someone says to you, "Have a good day!" just say, "Sorry, but I have other plans." It usually gets their attention.)

Saying goodbye extends to written communication as well. How do you end your letters, emails, text messages? When I write to a loved one, I often end with "Love, Melannie," "Love and prayers, Melannie," or "With much love, Melannie." With more formal correspondence I usually opt for the simple yet timeless "Sincerely."

Our partings from one another are significant. That's because we never know for sure when we will see each other again—or even *if* we will see each other again. When we experience the sudden or unexpected death of a friend or other loved one, often we immediately recall our last goodbye—which has now become our "final" goodbye.

Here's a touching story about a final goodbye. A couple had been married for over fifty years. When the wife crawled out of bed one morning, she said "Good morning" to her husband and gave him a kiss. They chatted for a moment. Then she got up while he stayed in bed. When he didn't appear in the kitchen a few minutes later as he always did, she went back to check on him and found him dead of a massive heart attack. Later, she remarked, "If I had known he was going to die that morning, I would have never stopped kissing him."

Because our partings are so important, we often mark them with ritualistic words (*goodbye... see ya... take care... I love you*) and with actions (kisses, hugs, pats on the back, handshakes, high fives, fist bumps). These words and gestures are all beautiful expressions of our love, respect, and appreciation for one another.

FOR REFLECTION

What are some of the ways you say goodbye to people?

How do you sign your emails, notes, or letters?

What have been some of the most memorable goodbyes you've experienced?

YOUTUBE VIDEO "Time to Say Goodbye," sung by Andrea Bocelli and Sarah Brightman

READERS' COMMENTS

"This reflection was filled with much wisdom regarding something we say almost daily. I liked what you wrote about 'Have a good day.' It is true that our attitude often does determine our day."

"When a person says, 'I won't say goodbye,' I usually say, I have no trouble saying goodbye because it means 'God be with you.'"

MY REFLECTIONS

18. Time for a Little Humor

Writer William Barclay said, "A gloomy Christian is a contradiction in terms." In other words, one hallmark of our Christian faith is joy—often expressed in laughter. We can laugh at the incongruities of life because we see them against the backdrop of God's great love for us, our fallen yet redeemed nature, and our belief in the ultimate triumph of good over evil. This reflection consists of humorous items that I hope will make you smile, laugh, or maybe even groan!

Fun with words:
My uncle named his pups Rolex and Timex. They're his watch dogs!

Stealing someone's coffee is called mugging.

Pasteurize: too far for you to see.

The other day I held the door open for a clown. It was a nice jester.

I've been to many places, but I've never been to Kahoots. Apparently, you can't go there alone. You have to be in Kahoots with someone.

I've also never been in Cognito. I hear no one recognizes you there.

I went to a psychic and knocked on her door. She asked, "Who is it?" So I left.

Okay, okay, I can hear you groaning, so let's move on to some...

Fun facts:
Only three countries don't use the metric system: Myanmar, Liberia, and the United States.

NFL Super Bowl referees also get Super Bowl rings.

Monaco's orchestra is bigger than its army. (There's something I really like about that fact... I wish other countries would follow their example!)

The word "strengths" is the longest word in the English language with only one vowel.

Candy Corn was originally called Chicken Feed.

One quarter of all your bones are located in your feet. (Let's hear it for our feet—and for all those foot doctors! Rah! Rah!)

And did you know that four out of three people struggle with math?

How about a few words of wisdom:

If you lend someone twenty dollars and never see that person again, it was probably worth it.

I went to buy some camouflage trousers yesterday, but I couldn't find any.

A Roman Legionnaire walks into a bar, holds up two fingers, and says, "I'll have five beers."

Save the earth. It's the only planet with chocolate.

The world is full of kind people. If you can't find one, be one.

And now, let's hear from our children:

On Father's Day, a single mom received a card from her eight-year-old son, who wrote: "Thank you for being the best two parents rolled into one!"

A father told his little girl that he had to go to work to get money for their vacation. The little girl ran into her bedroom and returned with her purse. She said to him, "I've been saving this money so you don't have to go to work anymore!"

On her little boy's first day of school, he was supposed to take a big yellow school bus. But his mother was leery of his being on that bus filled with all older kids. She told him she would drive him to school instead. But he told her, "Mommy, I've got to grow up and be a big boy one of these days." She smiled and said to him, "Thank you." A few minutes later, she watched her "big boy" get on the bus.

A little girl said, "If you want something expensive, ask your grandparents."

At bedtime, a little boy told his mother, "The monster that lives under my bed wants another cookie."

A mother was waiting to take her preschooler to school for the first time. She found him in the bathroom rubbing his arms and legs with her body lotion. He said to her, "I want to smell like you all day."

FOR REFLECTION

Did any of these make you smile?

What have you seen, heard, or read lately that made you smile or laugh?

YOUTUBE VIDEO

"We Walk by Faith," by Marty Haugen. We Christians should smile often because we believe in the Good News of the gospel. Check out this video: It captures the basis of our joy.

READERS' COMMENTS

"All the ones from the children made me laugh, but I was particularly struck by two: the little boy who gave his single mom that card thanking her for being the best two parents rolled into one, and the boy who was rubbing lotion on himself because he wanted to smell like his mom. Such wisdom from children!"

"I'm leaving for the Camino de Santiago in Spain in less than two weeks. The video was a 'wink' from God for me."

19. The Spirituality of Shredding

I've been doing a lot of shredding lately. I'm cleaning out some of my storage boxes. I don't want to leave all this stuff for someone else to have to deal with once I'm gone.

Most of my boxes are related to my years as a writer. I sold my first article on September 4, 1974. A writer remembers particulars like that. Other storage boxes are related to my retreat work and to the many talks I've given over the past four decades. I already pitched most of my teaching materials. One day (about twenty years ago) I realized I would never be teaching "The Rime of the Ancient Mariner" again. So, swoosh! I threw out all my teaching notes.

So, what am I shredding now? Here's a sampling:

1. Acceptance letters for articles I've sold.
2. Rejection letters for articles I didn't sell. Early in my writing career, I had hundreds of them. Now such correspondence is mostly electronic.
3. Correspondence with editors (over the years I've had many wonderful, talented, and helpful editors).

4. Duplicate copies of my unpublished poems, short stories, and articles.

The shredder we have here in our convent is a small one. I knew the volume of materials I was going to shred would demand a heavy-duty shredder. Fortunately, we have such a shredder at our provincial center. It shreds about ten to twelve sheets at a time. The manual claims it can shred even staples, paper clips, and credit cards—though I've never tested that claim.

The shredder sits in a small, windowless room in the basement. The only other things in the room are a two-drawer file cabinet (where the large garbage bags for the shredder are kept) and a small chair to put your stuff on while you stand and shred. When you turn the shredder on, it makes a loud growling sound—like a hungry dinosaur. When you begin feeding the paper into its jaws, the noise gets even louder as it devours your pages and then spits them into the attached garbage bag. Here are a few of my thoughts while shredding...

1. Shredding is a violent act. It entails a deafening racket and a brutal ferocity. It shreds paper into thin strips, making them indecipherable. Almost. We've all seen police dramas where forensic detectives painstakingly glue the shredded paper back together and solve the crime. But my shreds are destined for a recycling center.

2. Shredding can be a painful act. As I feed the machine, I glance at the pages and find myself protesting, "This is my life! These pages represent years of work and ministry. And in one instant, they're all gone! Wow!" At times I feel as if *I* am being shredded. So painful is shredding, I often refuse to look at the papers I'm feeding into the machine.

3. Shredding is a freeing act. Ironically, shredding also gives me a sense of satisfaction. It is a profound act of letting go. When I shred, I find myself saying, "I don't need this stuff anymore. That part of my life is over, is completed." I find this realization almost exhilarating.

4. Shredding is a grateful act. As I shred, I find myself thanking God for my life that these pages represent. "Thank you, God, for my editors... my readers... my students... for the gifts of writing and speaking... for your continuous inspiration... for my little successes... for my disappointments and failures which (I hope) have made me more humble and compassionate... Thank you, God, *for my whole life*, which has led me to where I am now and who I am today. Amen."

FOR REFLECTION

Have you ever used a shredder? If so, do you have any thoughts about shredding?

Have you ever felt God was asking you to let go of something? What was it, and what helped you to let go?

YOUTUBE VIDEO "Let Go," by Matt Hammitt

READERS' COMMENTS

"As a former student of yours, I am someone who learned 'The Rime of the Ancient Mariner' from you and benefited from those notes of yours that are now shredded. Though your notes may be gone, your work lives on in the minds and hearts of your grateful students."

"Thanks for bonding all of us together around a common experience of letting go, so aptly symbolized by our modern-day experience of shredding."

20. War and Peace

(Please note: This reflection deals with the very disturbing topic of war. Some may find it difficult to read. I understand. I found it difficult to write.)

The United States has three days set aside to honor its military personnel. Armed Forces Day, on the third Saturday in May, celebrates all active-duty service members. Veterans Day on November 11 honors all men and women who have ever served in the U.S. Military. And Memorial Day in May remembers and honors all those who died while serving in the Armed Forces. We honor them by praying for them, by holding memorial services, and by decorating their graves with flowers, wreaths, or small American flags. But the most important way we honor these men and women is by working for peace and justice—in our homes, workplaces, churches, local communities, country, and world.

"A Reflection on War and Peace"

Is there a celestial pub in heaven where all who died in battle gather from time to time to share their stories? If so, do they begin by telling the name of the war they fought in and the year they fell?

First Messenian War, 737 B.C.... Peloponnesian War, 428 B.C.... Zhao-Xiongnu War, 265 B.C.... Second Punic War, 212 B.C.... Fourth Crusade, 1203... Hundred Years' War, 1352... War of the Roses, 1481... Inca-Spanish War, 1532... Powhatan War, 1622... War of the Grand Alliance, 1690... War of the Spanish Succession, 1710... French and Indian War, 1762... Napoleonic Wars, 1805... Nanjing War, 1831... American Civil War, 1863... Paraguayan War, 1865... Anglo-Zulu War, 1879... First Sino-Japanese War, 1894... World War I, 1916... World War II, 1942... Korea, 1952... Vietnam, 1971... Iraq, 2004... Afghanistan, 2015... South Sudan, 2017... Ukraine, 2023... Israel-Gaza, 2024...

Do they share how they died and how old they were?

By hatchet, 21... nerve gas, 24... spear, 18... starvation, 30... cannonball, 25... dysentery, 19... shot down in our B22, 43... strafed by friendly fire, 23... bayonet, 16... sniper bullet to the neck, 19... incoming missile, 33... club, 15... grenade in our foxhole, 21... poisoned arrow, 20... firing squad, 25... suicide, 24... malaria, 27... went down with the Bismarck, 22... sword, 20... pneumonic plague, 25... roadside bomb, 30... drowning, 26... fire, 24... parachute didn't open, 20... bunker bombed, 32... drug overdose, 22... drone attack, 27... suffocation in a U-boat, 17... PTSD, 28...

Do they share where they died?

Wounded Knee... a rice paddy in Nam... Ulundi, South Africa... a frozen field outside Moscow... a MASH unit in Korea... Hiroshima... Dhauli Hills, India... somewhere in the Pacific... Jerusalem... Dresden... Crimea... Gettysburg... a roadside in Kabul... Pearl Harbor... Maya Lowlands... Wau, New Guinea... Normandy Beach... Mesopotamia... Concord,

Massachusetts... Marne River, France... Waterloo... Taiping, Malaysia... somewhere in the Alps... Anzio, Italy... POW prison in Vladivostok, Russia*...

And finally, what do these fallen warriors do before they disperse?

They raise their glasses of heavenly brew in honor of each other... they embrace their one-time enemies... they forgive again and again... they smile, they tease each other, they laugh... Then, locking their arms together, they join in one earnest and heartfelt prayer for the end of all wars on earth... and conclude their prayer by singing together in their own languages (which are now understood by all), "Let there be peace on earth, and let it begin with me."

* The soldier who died in a POW prison in Vladivostok, Russia, was my great-uncle, the younger brother of my Grandma Svoboda. As a young man, he was drafted into the Austro-Hungarian Army. He fought on the Siberian front, was taken prisoner, and shipped 7,000 miles from his home in Bohemia to this remote prison, where he died of some disease. His family didn't learn of his fate until several years after his death.

YouTube Video ⋘⋙ "Taps," performed in Arlington Cemetery (summer and winter)

"Let There Be Peace on Earth," sung by Voices of Hope Children's Choir (virtual choir)

Readers' Comments ⋘⋙

"Wow."

"Thank you for this thoughtful and wrenching reflection. May we all work for peace."

"Both videos really touched my heart. My husband was a proud Marine who served in Vietnam. He passed away two years ago from causes linked to Agent Orange. So, in my heart I feel he gave his life for his country."

MY REFLECTIONS

Winter

When it snows, you have two choices:
shovel or make snow angels.

ANONYMOUS

Winter is the season we behold the charms of
solemn majesty and naked grandeur.

JAMES ELLIS

Winter is a season of recovery
and preparation.

PAUL THEROUX

21. Winter: The Misunderstood Season

Some of us don't like winter. We see it as a season of ice and snow that disrupts our routine and puts a damper on our outdoor fun. (Unless, of course, you're an avid skier or snowboarder or you live in a place where you get very mild winters!) Have you ever noticed how some of the weather forecasters speak about winter? They say we will be *attacked* or *invaded* by a massive blast of Arctic air. Or a winter storm is going *to deliver a blow to the country's mid-section.* Poor winter! It desperately needs a better public relations firm!

Fortunately, there are some people who call winter (even the cold and snowy kind) "the most misunderstood season of all." They are quick to point out some of the beauties of the season. Artist Andrew Wyeth, for example, said, "I prefer winter and fall, when you feel the bone structure of the landscape—the loneliness of it, the dead feeling of winter. Something waits beneath it, the whole story doesn't show."

I know what he means. When I gaze at the frozen world, I can at first assume that everything is dead. But experience tells me the trees are not dead, they are dormant. Big difference. In winter, their life-sustaining sap is safely stored in their roots below and will rise again in spring. Centuries ago, the Persian poet Rumi wrote, "And don't think the garden loses ecstasy in winter. It's quiet, but the roots are down there riotous." Those bulbs now buried beneath the snow are holding last summer's sunlight. One day they will emerge as green shoots and burst forth into purple crocuses, red tulips, yellow daffodils, and pink hyacinths. And all those insect eggs carefully deposited under the bark of the trees or beneath the brown leaves on the forest floor—they, too, will emerge as creeping, crawling, buzzing insects of all kinds again. Winter, paradoxically, is the season of hope. You cradle hope in your heart despite the surrounding darkness and cold.

Another beauty of winter is gently falling snow. I like what Adrienne Ivey wrote about snow: "Everything is equal in snow: all trees, all lawns, all streets, all rooftops, all cars. Everything is white, white, white, as far as you can see." The manicured lawns and the neglected lawns look the same after a snowfall. So do the new car and the old jalopy. "Everything looks clean and fresh and unmarred by time or use. Snow... is a great leveler."

I also appreciate the quiet of a winter landscape. Snow muffles sound. Cars move almost silently on snow-covered streets. Windows in our homes are tightly shut so we barely hear any noise from outside. Snow mutes colors too. No bright flowers break the vast whiteness. When color does chance by in winter, it stops us in our tracks. Is there anything more breathtaking than a bright red cardinal flitting between the snow-laden branches of a tree?

Winter can encourage quiet reflection. It's an opportunity to not only *stay* inside, but to *go* inside oneself. Of all the seasons, says writer Shawna Lemay, "winter in particular sends us to the deep within our souls."

And finally, winter in the natural world teaches us how to live the winters of the spiritual world. This idea is expressed beautifully in the words of Sr. Joan Chittister, OSB: "Winter is about the fine art of loss and growth. Its lesson is clear: There is only one way out of struggle, and that is by going into the darkness, waiting for the light, and being open to new growth."

For Reflection

Did anything in this reflection touch your heart?

Do you like winter? Why or why not?

YouTube Video 〰️ "Winter Snow," written by Chris Tomlin and sung by Audrey Assad (several versions, with or without lyrics)

Readers' Comments 〰️

"Thank you for this lyrical tribute to one of my favorite seasons. At least it's my favorite until about Valentine's Day, when I start to hanker for a respite. For me, winter is a very beautiful and paradoxically a very fertile season—spiritually and poetically."

"I'm one of those who do NOT like winter. Never have. But I do appreciate the quiet introspection it provides."

My Reflections 〰️

22. Advent: A Celebration of Dreams and Promises

Advent is the season of the Church year that celebrates dreams and promises. The parched desert can burst into a field of poppies and forget-me-nots... Helpless little lambs can snuggle next to mighty ferocious lions... A wild, scrawny man dressed in animal hides and munching on grasshoppers can cry out in the wilderness,

"REPENT!" and large crowds can listen to his rantings and be radically changed... And a young girl, living unnoticed in Podunk, can say "yes" to an impossible Divine request and conceive a child who will turn her life and the whole world upside down.

The readings of Advent testify to all of these remarkable events. Maybe that's one reason we are so drawn to them. For they tell us: What you see is not all there is. What you think is the end is actually the beginning. What you desire in the deepest recesses of your heart can still be. The incredible things God has done in the past, God is doing in the present. Right now.

But there's a catch. God needs us. God needs us to help make these dreams come true, to help bring about these impossible promises. In the past, God needed an Isaiah to keep the vision of hope alive in God's people. God needed a John the Baptist to proclaim the message of returning to God. And God needed a Mary to dare to say "yes" to God's request as no other handmaid before her had ever done. So, Advent is not a time to set up permanent residence in comforting readings that promise a better future. No, it is a time to partner with God in the present to help bring about that better future for which we long.

How do we do this? The ways are countless and are limited only by our imagination and resolve. Many of these ways are mighty deeds, although they may seem pitifully small. Allow me to suggest a few.

+ The refrain for Advent is "Come, Lord Jesus." Perhaps we can make this refrain our mantra this Advent as we go about our day. When we first crawl out of bed in the morning, we can say, "Come, Lord Jesus, into my *entire* day. The easy parts, the nice parts, the fun parts. But also come into the messy parts, the unpleasant parts, the difficult parts." And when we crawl back into bed at night, we can say, "Come, Lord Jesus. Give me rest this night so I may partner with you again tomorrow."

+ Choose one way to make your small world a better place. Do this by following Jesus' way of unselfish loving. Speak kindly to others. *All* others. (Sometimes we're kinder to total strangers than we are to the people we live and work with every day.) Overlook some things. Go the extra mile. As St. John of the Cross says, where there is little or no love, put love and there will be love.

+ Find ways you can give your attention to someone overlooked, taken for granted, living on the margins. It can be a family member... co-worker... friend... neighbor... pastor... store clerk... overworked parent... shut-in... caregiver... stranger on the street. Simply ask yourself: Who is in need of a gentle word, a "thank you," a smile, a compliment, a note, a phone call, a visit, an offer to help?

And finally, my prayer for all of us this Advent is this:

Come, Lord Jesus! May the readings of Advent bring us great consolation. May they encourage us to dream for a better world. May they strengthen us to partner with you to bring about that better world we hope for. Give us a greater appreciation for the miracle of your life of selfless loving, a miracle we can share in every day. This Advent, rekindle in us the deepest longings of our hearts for love, peace, goodness, beauty, and truth. Come, Lord Jesus, come! Amen.

FOR REFLECTION

Did anything stand out for you in today's reflection?

Do you like the season of Advent? Why or why not?

YOUTUBE VIDEO "Beyond the Moon and Stars," by Dan Schutte

MY REFLECTIONS

 ## 23. Christmas: Small Is Beautiful

Christmas is a celebration of smallness. It proclaims that small is beautiful... the lowly is honorable... the ordinary is extraordinary.

Just look at the major characters in the Christmas story. First, there's Mary, a young girl (about thirteen years old) from a backwater town called Nazareth. Then there's Joseph, her husband, a lowly carpenter. And where is Jesus born? Not in the huge city of Rome or Jerusalem, but (as the Christmas carol says), in the *little* town of Bethlehem. And our first glimpse of "the Son of the Most High" is not a king robed in regal attire and seated on a throne but a tiny, squirming newborn wrapped in swaddling clothes and lying in a feeding trough. The first visitors to pay him homage are not Roman rulers or dignitaries but a scruffy band of ordinary shepherds.

Small. Lowly. Ordinary. These are not exactly the watchwords of our day. On the contrary, ours is a world that says bigger is better, a culture that overuses words such as *mega, super, ultra*. Ours is a world where, for many, fame and fortune are the main goals in life. Ours is a world that glorifies power and rewards arrogance. Perhaps we need, more than ever, to hear this particular message of Christmas: the call to celebrate the small.

Didn't the adult Jesus show us precisely how to do this? He chooses as his disciples ordinary individuals. Although he preached to all, he directs his message particularly to the poor and marginalized. He compares the kingdom of God to a *tiny* mustard seed, and he tells his followers to become "as little children." He says, "What you did to the *least*, you did to me." And finally, "I am meek and humble of heart."

This appreciation of smallness and lowliness will instill in us respect for the many forms smallness may take in our lives: inexperience, vulnerability, imperfection, powerlessness. It will call forth respect for "small people" in our midst: the unborn, children, the elderly, the refugee, the poor. We might ask ourselves questions such as these: How concerned am I for the children of our world? How do I respond to the homeless, the sick, the physically or mentally challenged, those who are denied their legal rights, the incarcerated?

Other questions to ask: How do I respond when I experience smallness and lowliness within myself? Am I patient with my human failings? When I feel powerless, do I throw up my hands in despair—or do I reach out my hand to the ever-ready hand of God? Do I respect and cherish the ordinary, the familiar? Do I regularly thank God for the beauties of my everyday life?

St. Paul not only accepted his lowliness, he boasted about it: "I will boast of things that show my weakness." How could he do this? Because he believed those words of Jesus: "My grace is sufficient for you, for power is made perfect in weakness."

Let us pray... Heavenly Father, your Son Jesus came into our world in a quiet and unassuming way. He taught us to be attentive to the divine within our midst—especially in the small, lowly, and ordinary. Help us to see these qualities as central to the Christmas story. Give us a greater awareness of the blessings of our everyday life: the familiar individuals we interact with every day... our commonplace surroundings... our quotidian activities... our usual deeds... our ordinary joys and struggles. Help us to accept our own failings and weaknesses, relying on your own strength within us. We ask for these graces knowing that your power and goodness are at work within us and in our entire Earth community. Amen.

FOR REFLECTION

Did anything touch your heart in this reflection?

To what extent have you bought into the culture that says bigger is better, fame and fortune are the goals in life, or power is everything?

YouTube Video "Mary, Did You Know?" Sing-along video by Pentatonix or versions by Carrie Underwood or Michael English

READERS' COMMENTS

"Your reflections often bring me smiles, deep thought, appreciation for all God has given me, and a realization of ways I can give."

"Your music choices are always the frosting on the cake. They add measurably to your reflections."

"Appreciation of the small things in life is one of my most valuable takeaways from living through the pandemic."

24. The Magic and Power of Reading

I once saw a poster that said, "If you can read this, thank a teacher." I thought of my first grade teacher, Miss Enniert, at James A. Garfield School. Although I can't even remember what she looked like, I realize she was the first person who taught me how to read. She developed in me that incredible skill that eventually turned into a lifelong passion. And so today I publicly say: "Thank you, Miss Enniert, for teaching me how to read!"

The ability to read is a marvelous gift. But what exactly is reading? Simply put, reading is a complex process of decoding signs or symbols in order to derive meaning from them. Imagine if you couldn't read and you saw a book for the first time. What would you see when you opened it? A bunch of little black squiggly marks on every page. When I was in Korea, I toured an elementary school with a library that had over 10,000 books—all in Korean, of course. I suddenly realized I wouldn't be able to read a single book in that library, because I didn't know the code to decipher those squiggly marks.

Reading is shaped by the reader's prior knowledge, experience, attitude, and culture. That's why Edmund Wilson could declare: "No two persons ever read the same book." When we read, we usually read silently and without forming the words with our lips. But in the fourth century, St. Augustine remarked on St. Ambrose's "unusual" way of reading: He read silently and without moving his lips! This was the first time Augustine had encountered such a thing.

Here are ten facts about reading that are worth pondering:

1. Worldwide, people spend an average of 6.5 hours a week reading.

2. In the United States, 63% of the adult population of prisoners are functionally illiterate, and 85% of all juveniles who come into contact with the juvenile court system are functionally illiterate.

3. The Penguin paperback was created in 1935 to make books as affordable as cigarettes.

4. Throughout history, for religious or political reasons, books have been censored or burned.

5. Ray Bradbury, author of *Fahrenheit 451*, said, "There are worse crimes than burning books. One of them is not reading them." His classic book tells of a futuristic world in which all books are burned. Fahrenheit 451 is the temperature at which book paper catches fire.

6. Half of all the books sold today are to people over the age of 45. The number of books read by adults over 65 is higher than any other age group.

7. Women buy 68% of all the books sold. But 80% of books published in the United States are written by men.

8. The average adult reads 200 to 400 words per minute.

9. The most popular time of day for reading is before bed.
10. Reading and writing are brain-stimulating activities that have been shown to slow down cognitive decline.

Many beautiful words have been used to describe the magic and power of reading. Two of my favorites are these:

> Elizabeth Hardwick, literary critic, novelist, short story writer: "The greatest gift is a passion for reading. It is cheap, it consoles, it distracts, it excites, it gives you knowledge of the world and experience of a wider kind. It is a moral illumination."

> Mary Schmich, Pulitzer Prize–winning journalist: "Reading is a discount ticket to everywhere."

If you are still reading this, thank a teacher! And thank God for your good fortune to be a reader!

FOR REFLECTION

What role does reading play in your everyday life? In your spiritual life?

Why are you reading this book?

YOUTUBE VIDEO "Seek Ye First," by Karen Lafferty, sung by the Maranatha Singers

READERS' COMMENTS

"To me, reading is everything. It is my livelihood. I work as an editor for a publishing company. Reading is also important for my spiritual life. The Bible and many other books keep me on my journey."

"What a wonderful topic! My parents taught me to read. They bought subscriptions to children's magazines and took me to the library. As a high school student, my world was widened thanks to teachers like Sister Kathleen who had us reading classics by Antoine de Saint-Exupéry, Thomas Merton, and many others."

MY REFLECTIONS

25. Twenty Quotations for Hard Times

As we all know, life is not easy. On the contrary, life can be extremely challenging at times. But it is primarily through life's challenges that we can grow in virtues such as love, patience, understanding, compassion, humility, and trust in our loving God. Here are twenty quotations that have encouraged me during hard times in my life. Perhaps some of them might speak to you too.

1. Good is never done except at the expense of those who do it. *St. John Henry Newman*
2. Do not let what you cannot do interfere with what you can do. *John Wooden, basketball coach*
3. Failures aren't failures if you learn from them. *Anne Morrow Lindbergh*

4. There are no shortcuts to anyplace worth going.
   Beverly Sills, opera singer
5. When God closes a door, God opens a window. *Gerald Bath*
6. God gives every bird its food, but God does not throw it into the nest. *Josiah Holland*
7. The rower reaches the shore, partly by pulling, partly by letting go. *Egyptian proverb*
8. The person who makes no mistakes never makes anything. *English proverb*
9. To live is to adapt. *Johann Wolfgang von Goethe*
10. The greatest discovery of my generation is that human beings can alter their lives by altering their attitude. *William James*
11. The lowest ebb is the turn of the tide. *Anonymous*
12. Pessimists complain about the wind. Optimists hope it will change. Realists adjust the sails. *William Arthur Ward*
13. There are some things you learn best in calm, and some in storm. *Willa Cather*
14. Where you stumble and fall, there you will find pure gold. *Carl Jung*
15. No Christian escapes a taste of the wilderness on the way to the Promised Land. *Evelyn Underhill*
16. For every complex problem, there's a solution that's clear, simple, and wrong. *H.L. Mencken*
17. Adversity introduces us to ourselves. *George W. Bush*
18. See all, overlook much, improve a little. *Pope John XXIII*
19. Love and suffering are the primary spiritual teachers. *Richard Rohr*
20. Life is never so bad at its worst that it is impossible to live; it is never so good at its best that it is easy to live. *Anonymous*

FOR REFLECTION ⟨⟨⟨

Do any of the quotes speak to you today? If so, which one(s) and why?

Do you disagree with any of the quotes? Or would you modify any of them? Why?

Do you have a favorite quote that helps you during difficult times?

YOUTUBE VIDEO ⟨⟨⟨ "Peace Is Flowing like a River," by Carey Landry; video by Steve Politte

READERS' COMMENTS ⟨⟨⟨

"I like #2: 'Do not let what you cannot do interfere with what you can do.' I'm learning to play the guitar, and my fingers don't want to do what they're supposed to do. But I've sworn to keep at it, if it takes me years!"

"All the quotes are lovely and very timely. My 90-year-old mother has a terminal illness and will be leaving us soon. I especially liked #17: 'The rower reaches the shore, partly by pulling, partly by letting go.' And #19: 'Love and suffering are the primary spiritual teachers.'"

MY REFLECTIONS ⟨⟨⟨

26. What Advice Would St. Joseph Give Us?

One of the central figures of the Advent and Christmas seasons is St. Joseph, the husband of Mary. Based on Scripture, what advice would Joseph give to us? I'm suggesting these three pieces of advice.

The first one is this: *Remember, God works marvels through ordinary people.* Joseph was a fairly ordinary person. John's gospel doesn't even mention him. Mark's gospel mentions him only in passing, calling Jesus "the carpenter's son." In Luke's gospel the focus is on Mary, with Joseph taking a back seat. Only in Matthew's gospel is Joseph given any real attention. Yet, he utters not a single word in any of the gospels.

Joseph was content to play a supporting role in the great drama of salvation. He did not have to be center stage. He embraced being ordinary, for the truth is, God works most often through ordinary people. In the gospels we see God working through a young peasant girl named Mary, a group of lowly shepherds, a handful of mangy fishermen, an assortment of devoted women, a vertically challenged tax collector, a Roman soldier with a sensitive heart, and a destitute widow down to her last two coins. St. Joseph reminds us that being faithful to God is far more important than being rich, famous, or extraordinary.

The second piece of advice is this: *Keep trusting in God no matter what—even when your life is turned upside down.* The Annunciation turned Mary's life upside down. It also turned Joseph's life upside down. Mary's pregnancy initially caused Joseph deep anguish, for he knew the child she was carrying was not his. In these circumstances, he honestly didn't know what to do. His faith gave him essentially two options: Divorce Mary or have her stoned to death for infidelity.

As Joseph tossed and turned in bed at night, an angel appeared and told him that Mary's child was "the Son of the Most High." The angel then presented Joseph with a third option: "Marry Mary and raise the child as your own." Joseph believed what had been revealed to him and did as the angel urged. But even after deciding to marry Mary, things were not easy for him. He was not given a manual (or an app!) on "How to Raise a Messiah." No, he had to learn on the job through trial and error, one day at a time. Like us, Joseph learned how to live by living. Like us, he had to trust in God—especially when the path into the future was unclear.

The third piece of Joseph's advice might be this: *Life is not easy, but God is with us through all our difficulties.* The gospels make it clear that Joseph did not have a carefree life. The trip to Bethlehem was no pleasant excursion into the countryside; it was an arduous trek through inhospitable lands with a young wife who was nine months pregnant. The flight into Egypt had to be traumatic too. We can catch a glimpse of what this upheaval must have meant for Joseph and Mary when, in the news, we see the weary and terror-stricken faces of today's refugees. Added to these hardships were the daily trials of a working man trying to scratch out a living for his wife and son in a poor country that had been economically drained by a foreign military power.

During this season and all the seasons of our life, may we learn from the example of St. Joseph. This ordinary and unassuming man, in all the circumstances of his life, held fast to his belief in the God of absolute goodness and infinite love.

FOR REFLECTION

Of the three lessons Joseph teaches us, which one do you need most in your life today? Why?

Can you think of other lessons Joseph can teach us?

YouTube Video ~~~ "Joseph's Song," by Michael Card

Readers' Comments ~~~

"Listening to 'Joseph's Song' never fails to bring tears to my eyes. Joseph's prayer in this song is such a good prayer for all of us: 'Father, show me how to fit into this plan of yours.' And I would add, 'Help me to fulfill your purpose for my life even if I don't see where I fit into your plan.'"

"Michael Card's song begs us to reflect on the ordinary doing the extraordinary, on the trusting soul becoming the trustworthy one, and on the real difference between presents and presence."

My Reflections ~~~

 ## 27. A Prayer for When Life Doesn't Make Sense

Sometimes life is good and faith is easy. Choose your image: the seas of your life are calm... the components of your life are gently falling into place... the people around you are agreeable and kind.

But sometimes life doesn't make sense and faith is tough. Things happen (or a single BIG thing happens) that (choose your image):

knocks you off your feet... causes you to cry out, "No! No!"... raises the nagging question, "How could a good God allow This Terrible Thing to happen?" This is a prayer for times like that.

Prayer for When Life Doesn't Make Sense

I don't get it, God... I just don't understand... And I WANT to understand... I NEED to understand.

Just explain it to me. Help me to see how This Thing makes sense. I think I could accept it if it somehow made sense. If it was logical... fair... reasonable. If I could see a PURPOSE in it. Or, better yet, if I could see some GOOD in it... Some GOOD that This Thing will bring about... Some GOOD that outweighs the bad I can only see now... Some GOOD that makes This Thing not only understandable, but acceptable.

I'm hanging on, God. I'm hanging on to the end of a branch, and I'm pretty high up in the tree too... (Or) I'm clinging to my capsized canoe and being tossed up and down by the waves... (Or) I'm reciting, "The Lord is my shepherd the Lord is my shepherd the Lord is my shepherd," words that used to give me comfort but now seem empty.

All I have left right now, God, is faith. Pure faith. Or (more accurately) all I have left right now is my trust in you... in your wisdom... your goodness... your love. I'm trying to trust in you, God, but frankly, my trust is wearing thin. Very thin. So thin I sometimes wonder if it exists at all.

So, here I am, God, begging, as I sometimes must do. I'm begging you to help me. Help me to hang on. Give me the strength to face This Thing... to deal with This Thing... to endure This Thing. And give me direction. Help me to see what This Thing might mean for me... what it might be asking of me... what it might be calling me to do. As I ask for these things, I am thinking of Jesus, your Son.

For in Gethsemane, Jesus, too, faced a BIG Thing that made no sense... that knocked him to his knees: his looming death by horrific crucifixion. It was there among the old, gnarled olive trees that he uttered words that I imagine were similar to the words I am crying now: "Not this, God!... Not this!... Anything but this!" Jesus begged you, his Father, "Let this cup pass from me." But then he added those words I am trying to make my own: "Not as I will, but as you will" (Matthew 26:39)... Jesus was clinging to the only thing he had left: his unconditional trust in you. Because his trust in you was so deep, he could cry out with a loud voice even while hanging on the cross, "Father, into your hands I commend my spirit" (Luke 23:46).

*Loving God, I beg you now. Help me to make Jesus'
words my own. Help me to believe This Thing is in your
hands... and so am I... and so are all of us. Amen.*

FOR REFLECTION
Toward the end of the video, you see a flock of birds flying closely together. They do this for safety as they migrate. That image raises these questions:

Has anyone ever been a sanctuary for you during your lifetime? When and how?

Have you ever been a sanctuary for someone else? When and how?

YOUTUBE VIDEO "Sanctuary," by Carrie Newcomer

READERS' COMMENTS
"I love this reflection today, and I will pass it on to someone I know who is going through one of those Big Things you talk about."

"Thank you for the song 'Sanctuary'—for the word itself and its dynamic meaning. Sanctuary: seeking it when needed and being it for others when they need it."

MY REFLECTIONS

28. A Few Words about Complaining

Are you a complainer? Or do you follow of the rule of "If you don't have something nice to say, don't say anything at all"? Or do you think complaining can be a good thing sometimes? To get help answering these questions, I'm turning to an article in *Notre Dame Magazine* (Autumn 2022) by Andrew Santella entitled "Eight Complaints." Here's what some famous people have said about complaining.

Aristotle claimed that complaining was "typical of the weaker sex." (I suspect many women would complain about his words!) Kant wrote that complaining was "unworthy" of the dignified, virtuous person. (Does that mean saints never complain?) And Nietzsche wrote: "Complaining is never of any use." (Really, Friedrich?)

In the twelfth century, a French Benedictine monk helped support his monastery by writing songs about things that annoyed him. What things? Here are a few: "I can't stand a long wait... or a priest who lies... or the hoarse man who tries to sing... or too much water in too little wine... or little meat in a large dish." (Do any of these seem timeless?)

What is the oldest surviving *customer* complaint? It was made in Mesopotamia around 1750 BC and still survives on a cuneiform tablet. A dissatisfied customer named Nanni wrote to a supplier called Ea-nasir who not only delivered the wrong grade of copper to Nanni, he delivered it late. Nanni wrote: "What do you take me for that you treat me so badly? I have sent messengers to collect my money, but you have sent them back empty-handed." Some of us can identify with his frustration.

Why is complaining so universal? Writes Santella, "Because there has always been so much to complain about." He dubs New York City (where he lives) the "World Capital of Complaining." He lists some of the most frequent complaints: high rent, slow subways, rogue car alarms, and illegal parking. Democracies "thrive on complaints"—as letters to the editor or posts on social media affirm. (I bet Putin doesn't get many complaints.)

Can complaining be a good thing? Santella says that psychologists tend to be ambiguous on the benefits of complaining: "It can be healthy, they say, except when it's unhealthy." The truth is, sometimes we just need to vent. And whining, complaining, moaning, or groaning are ways we vent. Hopefully, we all have a few trusted friends who are willing to listen to our complaints. So, it's okay to whine—from time to time. But if our whining is chronic, then that's not healthy. At the same time, we must remember that some serious complaints have led to serious changes for the better. Says Santella, "Female suffrage, the Civil Rights Movement, and South-Africa's anti-apartheid campaign all grew from the seed of complaint about wrongs needing correction."

Have you noticed that there's a lot of complaining in the Bible too? The classic example is the Chosen People. After their miraculous deliverance from the slavery of Egypt, what do they do? They grumble about all kinds of things—like the manna, the bread from heaven, "not tasting quite right." Others in the Bible complain. Moses even complains about the Israelites complaining! Job and Jeremiah both wish they had never been born. And we have an entire book in the Bible called "Lamentations."

At the end of his article, Santella notes: "Complaint does not equal unhappiness." That French monk who wrote all those songs of complaint "seems to have been very jovial—and a pretty welcome party guest."

FOR REFLECTION

On a scale of one to ten (with one meaning "I never complain" and ten meaning "I always complain"), how would you rate yourself?

What are your most frequent complaints?

Can you give other examples of how a "seed of complaint" led to a better world?

Do you complain to God? Why or why not?

YOUTUBE VIDEO "Thank You Lord," by Don Moen (with lyrics)

READERS' COMMENTS

"My complaining score is three. My most common complaints are business expectations falling short. I share my disappointment with the owner in hopes of a better outcome. I share my frustrations with God. His ways are not always my ways."

"I'm generally successful at keeping my complaints below a five. After all, with good health, retirement on the horizon, a loving wife and adult

children, and a two-year-old grandson, I truly have much to be grateful
for and little to complain about."

MY REFLECTIONS

29. To the Birds at My Feeders

Come, all ye birds, to my bird feeders! I've put out some black oil sunflower seeds just for you. The kind I know you like.

Come, Cardinals, and delight me with your splash of brilliant red or (if you're a lady) your subtle earth tones with just a peek of muted red around your wings. Come, you little Black-Capped Chickadees, you "darlings of the backyard feeder," and steal a single seed and flit away to a nearby tree to enjoy it. Evidently, you are too shy to dine at my table, but you partake of my feast nonetheless.

Come, you bright Goldfinch. I've put out fresh thistle seeds for you. Come, Tufted Titmouse or (if there's more than one of you) Titmice! I've heard you are so bold you'll pluck hairs from a sleeping dog or cat to use as a lining for your nest. Such courage requires hearty nourishment.

Come, Woodpeckers clad in your stylish red, white, and black. I've put out some peanuts and suet for you. Come, Blue Jay. Though you are rather large, you still partake in avian gracefulness. Though you seem crabby most days, too, your pretty blue hue has persuaded me to include you on my guest list. But please watch your table manners. And don't chase away my other, smaller guests.

And you, my lovely orange-and-black Baltimore Orioles, I know sunflower seeds aren't your thing. So, I've put half an orange on the feeder just for you. And although I haven't spotted you yet this year, I know you're apt to show up as you did last year and the year before. You've probably already made reservations for a nearby tree in which to fashion your hanging nest.

And what about you, Ms. Chipmunk? Although you can't reach my table (it's not that you haven't tried!), you are welcome to partake of the seeds that the birds, in their eagerness for my feast, scatter on the ground below. I've seen you scooting away from my feeder, your tail straight up in the air, and your cheeks bulging with seeds. You are welcome beneath my table. I'm a sucker for cuteness.

And Mr. Squirrel, you, too, lust after my bird feeder fare. And though not a bird, you are God's creature too (as my mother used to say when your kin stole seeds from her feeder years ago). But sunflower seeds are expensive these days, and I can't afford to officially welcome you to my feeder. That's why, if I see you hanging from my feeder (often in very imaginative and acrobatic ways), I'll tap hard on the window and shoo you away. But I know (and you know) I can't be watching every minute.

So, welcome, birds. And chipmunks too. But I have to draw the line somewhere. And so I do—at squirrels, raccoons, and deer. Your appetites are just too big for my modest budget.

So, all ye Birds at my bird feeders, I'm happy you enjoy my feast. But I enjoy *my feast* too: the feast of beholding all of you!

For Reflection

Do you have a bird feeder? If so, what do you enjoy most about having one? What do you enjoy least?

Do birds nourish your spiritual life? If so, how?

YouTube Video "Bird Song Opera," by ShakeUp Music

Readers' Comments

"We continue to TRY to rig a bird feeder that will feed the BIRDS and not the big, fat squirrel. Honestly, you would think a squirrel with a belly that big could never leap from tree to bird feeder like he (or she) does. Sometimes the squirrel topples the whole feeder, spilling the seeds for EVERYONE. There must be a life lesson in there somewhere."

"Blue Jays are always welcome in my yard because of their beauty and courage. I have watched them chase hawks from the trees near my birdbath. They always alert the smaller, pretty songbirds that a hawk is around. I think of them as God's little sentries."

My Reflections

30. Singing Is Good for You

I like to sing. I always have. As little girls, my sister and I used to sing duets in harmony. Our favorites were "Harbor Lights" and "You Belong to Me." I sang in our parish children's choir, in my high school glee club, and now in the choir here at our provincial center. That's why a 2023 article in *The Washington Post* by Alexandra Moe caught my attention. She says recent research shows that singing is good for you—especially singing with others.

The article began with a London woman named Hazel Hardy. Every Wednesday, she travels for choir practice to a church on the other side of town. Her choir is not an ordinary choir, though. All the members are individuals familiar with cancer—as patients (like Hazel), caregivers, and oncologists. They come together not to talk about cancer but to sing and have a little fun.

After rehearsals, some singers provide a saliva sample to researchers who are studying whether singing affects the choir members' health and mood. It does. In fact, there is a growing body of research that points to the physical and mental benefits of singing with others. Singing together can reduce stress hormones and increase cytokines, proteins that can boost the body's ability to fight serious illness.

Other studies have shown that singing can lessen anxiety, stimulate memory for those with dementia, increase lung capacity, and ease postpartum depression. Stanley Thurston, founder of the Heritage Signature Chorale in Washington, DC, says, "Choirs are large families." They promote social bonding and also give the members a sense of achievement after months of working on a beautiful musical work.

In 2019, some fifty-four million Americans sang in choirs. Those who did tended to be "more optimistic, more likely to vote, less lonely, possessed stronger relationships, and were more likely to contribute to their communities than non-singers." Singing can be calming too. Lullabies soothe the baby, yes, but they can also soothe the singer.

But what if you can't sing? "If you can breathe and make sound, you can sing and receive its benefits," says researcher Suzi Zumpe. She incorporates music in her work to help relieve breathlessness and anxiety for people with long Covid.

The first song Hazel Hardy's choir learned was "I Can See Clearly Now." But their real "showstopper" was "I Will Survive" by Gloria Gaynor, which describes cancer as unwelcome and demands that it makes its exit. (The video can be found on YouTube.) Says Stanley Thurston, singing "affects the way you feel about being alive. It's an expression of, 'Yes, I am here.' It feeds my soul."

Let me conclude with two good quotes about singing by two individuals separated by many centuries. St. Augustine: "To sing is to pray twice." And Aretha Franklin: "The only thing better than singing is more singing."

FOR REFLECTION

Do you sing in a choir, with another group, or at Mass?

Do you ever sing when you pray?

Have you experienced any benefits from singing?

Would you add any other benefits you've experienced by singing— either alone or with others?

YOUTUBE VIDEO "I Will Survive," sung by Gloria Gaynor. Click on the version where she sings with patients and supporters at Miami's Nicklaus Children's Hospital. She has adapted the words of her original song to "I Will Survive Bald, Brave, Beautiful®."

"I sang in the children's choir at our church. I sang 'Hail Mary, Gentle Woman' as a lullaby to my daughter when I was a new mom. I don't know if my singing calmed her down, but it helped me. I always thought singing was good for our well-being. It's good to know someone has confirmed it."

"I sing to our dog while I'm driving with the windows wide open as we careen happily up and down the roads. Our favorite song is '[I Love You] A Bushel and a Peck.' I sing in the shower and while working outside. But I am not a good singer at all, so in church I sing in a softer voice."

MY REFLECTIONS

Spring

To plant a garden is to believe in tomorrow.
AUDREY HEPBURN

Nothing ever seems impossible in Spring.
L.M. MONTGOMERY

*Happiness? The color of it
must be spring green.*
FRANCES MAYES

31. The Turtle Story: A Reflection for Holy Week and Easter

Writer Barbara Brown Taylor is an Episcopal priest, professor, and theologian. She lives on a small farm in Georgia with her husband, Ed. In her book *Learning to Walk in the Dark*, she tells this true story, a story I find very appropriate for Holy Week and Easter.

A few years back, Taylor and her husband were exploring the dunes on Cumberland Island off the coast of Georgia. Ed was looking for fossilized shark teeth. She was looking for sand spurs so she wouldn't step on any. This meant they were both looking down at their feet when suddenly they came upon a huge loggerhead turtle in the sand. The turtle was alive—barely. Her shell was too hot to touch. Instantly, they knew what had happened.

During the night, the turtle had come ashore to lay her eggs. When she finished her task, she looked around for the brightest horizon to lead her back to the sea. But mistaking the lights on the mainland for the sky reflected in the ocean, she had gone the wrong way. Now her flippers were buried in sand and she was stuck, half-baked in the noonday sun.

Taylor began to bury the turtle in cool sand while Ed ran to the nearest ranger station. She writes, "An hour later the turtle was on her back with tire chains around her front legs, being dragged behind a park service Jeep back toward the ocean." The poor turtle's mouth was filled with sand and her head was so bent Taylor feared her neck would break. But it didn't. When they got to the edge of the water, the three undid the chains, gently flipped the turtle right side up, and "watched as she lay motionless in the surf."

Gradually, the waves around her began to bring her back to life. Then the waves lifted her up, and she pushed off with her back legs and swam back "into the water that was her home." Taylor concludes: "Watching her swim slowly away after her nightmare ride through the dunes, I noted that it is sometimes hard to tell whether you are being killed or saved by the hands that turn your life upside down."

Some thoughts about this story...

Paradoxes: In the process of bringing new life into the world, the turtle almost loses her own life... To be saved, she had to undergo a nightmare of a journey that almost killed her.

The story makes me think of all those individuals undergoing "nightmare journeys" of their own—painful surgery, chemotherapy, rehab of all kinds. At times they, too, must wonder: Am I being killed or saved?

And what about Jesus? His life was turned upside down in Gethsemane. His crucifixion raises a million questions like these: Why did he have to die? How was he able to endure the injustice of it all, the mockery, the beatings, those nails, the hanging in the hot sun for three hours? And where was God, Abba, during all of this?

I pray for those people right now who are enduring their own passions—those suffering from wars, famine, violence, racial injustice, human trafficking, religious persecution, natural disasters, and the list goes on and on. And I beg God to be with them in their suffering... and to move the hearts of good and generous people (like us!) to give them aid and comfort... and to move my own heart to reach out to someone in need today.

And I pray for a greater realization of the power of the Resurrection in our lives as we make our journey back to our true home, the open sea of God's mercy and love.

FOR REFLECTION

Have you ever had an experience like the loggerhead turtle in this story—a near-death experience that turned out to be a new-life experience?

Or an experience where goodness was born from apparent evil?

YOUTUBE VIDEO "We Remember," by Marty Haugen – video by Lorna Yumul Santos

READERS' COMMENTS

"What a beautiful story! Pain for new life. A wonderful analogy for the Resurrection."

"I was experiencing a sense of aloneness as a retired priest living in a rectory. Then I suffered an unexpected stroke. The stroke necessitated a move to a wonderful community in an assisted living facility. God's plan always seems to be one up on ours."

MY REFLECTIONS

32. Interview with a Hopeful Vegan

The virtue of hope is not a passive virtue. It calls us to take specific actions in the present to help bring about the better world we are hoping for in the future. Meet Sister Ann Marie Teder, a good friend of mine, who decided several years ago to go vegan. Recently, she prepared a vegan dinner for the two of us: lentil soup, tomato-basil-avocado sandwich, fruit salad, and (for dessert) eggless ginger snaps and non-dairy ice cream. It was delicious! Afterward, I interviewed her for this reflection.

What is a vegan? A vegan is a person who does not eat or use animal products. (That means no meat, fish, eggs, cheese, and no use of leather goods, etc.)

Why do people in general go vegan? Most become vegan for their own health, for animal welfare, for the environmental impact, and for the poor.

Why did YOU make this choice? When I ate outside on our deck near the bird feeder, I used to wonder if the birds knew I was eating a bird (chicken). At one point, I decided if I loved animals, I had to stop eating them. So, on Ash Wednesday 2016, I gave up meat for good.

Later that year, I learned about factory farming. After watching undercover videos and seeing the suffering of animals—including fish—I knew I needed to make a change. Most meat, dairy, and eggs sold in the United States come from factory farms. I felt a disconnect between my values and what I was eating. So, in Lent 2017 I went vegan. What I didn't expect was the peace I felt afterward. By this single decision, I can spare animals, help save the environment, lessen poverty, and improve my health. Another thing: It's always easier to ask *others* to change—sign a petition, vote, etc. Going vegan means *I* change instead of asking animals to suffer and die for my sake.

You mentioned the suffering of animals. Don't animal welfare laws (at least in this country) protect animals?   Animals used for food and other products are exempt from those laws. Birds aren't even covered under "humane slaughter laws," laws which are often not enforced.

Why not change the laws and raise animals humanely?   We should change the laws. But even if we cut down all the forests, we wouldn't have enough land to raise animals humanely. The real problem is our demand. Factory farms were created in response to our great demand for certain foods.

Do you get proper nutrition eating vegan?   Yes. The health benefits of a vegan diet are well documented. Eating animals and animal products is actually unhealthy. But if you decide to go vegetarian or vegan, tell your doctor. You may need a B-12 supplement, for example, or iron.

Are your eating choices expensive and/or time-consuming to implement?   Individual items can cost a bit more, but vegan meals are overall equivalent to or less expensive than non-vegan meals. Preparation time is about the same. If you live with omnivores, you need not make separate meals. You can make "accidentally vegan" dishes (like pasta with marinara sauce) or ones where you can remove portions for the vegans and then add the animal products afterward for the omnivores.

Do you have any regrets about going vegan?   I have only one. It's summarized in this quote: "Dear animals, I'm sorry it took me so long."

Is there anything else you would like to say about this choice you've made?   Being vegan has stretched me in a good way. I'm still learning about it and transitioning. I'll leave you with this quote by Colleen Patrick-Goudreau: "May our daily choices be a reflection of our deepest values, and may we use our voices to speak for those who need us most, those who have no voice, those who have no choice."

For Reflection

Is there anything in this interview that stood out for you?

Are you vegan or vegetarian? If so, what motivates you?

Do you ever consider your eating habits as part of your spiritual life?

YouTube Video "Bless the Beasts and the Children," by The Carpenters (with lyrics)

Readers' Comments

"I enjoyed reading about Sr. Annie's journey. I have been lacto-ovo vegetarian since the early '80s. I have not ventured into being a vegan, but I quit fish a few years ago. Congrats, Sr. Annie, on your sensitivity to animals as a reason for your decision. I need to learn from you."

"A beautiful video. We must be a voice for the voiceless. Great information to share on the vegan lifestyle as it helps us manage and prevent many chronic diseases."

My Reflections

33. God as a Woman in Labor

Lauren Winner, an ordained Episcopal priest, has written a book entitled *Wearing God: Clothing, Laughter, Fire, and Other Overlooked Ways of Meeting God.* Winter reminds us that all the ways we describe God are inadequate. God is beyond anything we could ever say. Yet, the Bible offers us many images or metaphors of God that can give us insights into who God is. Some Christians, however, focus on only a few of those biblical images of God, such as king, shepherd, father. By doing so, says Winner, we "have truncated our relationship with the divine."

Winner's book explores scriptural images of God often overlooked: God as clothing... bread... smell... laughter... a laboring woman. In this reflection, we will explore the image of God as a woman in labor.

This image is found in Isaiah 42:14, where God says through the prophet: "For a long time I have kept silent, I have said nothing, holding myself back; Now I cry out like a woman in labor, gasping and panting." Isaiah wrote these words when a significant part of the Judean population was living in exile in Babylon, with little hope of returning home. In the wake of such a catastrophe, Isaiah was assuring the people that God was one with them in their pain—a pain that would lead to birth and new life.

Other Scripture passages repeat this image of God as a laboring woman. St. Augustine interpreted Psalm 110:3 in these words: God says, "From my womb before the morning star I have brought thee forth." You mean God has a womb? Later Isaiah gives the people these tender words from God: "Can a mother forget her infant, be without tenderness for the child of her womb? Even should she forget, I will never forget you" (Isaiah 49:15).

Some might be disturbed by these images of God as a laboring woman groaning, bleeding, and writhing in pain. But Winner suggests that such images tell us "God chooses to participate in the work of new creation with bellowing and panting." And God, especially through Jesus, continues to nourish us with his own body as a woman nourishes her child with her own body.

These images of God gave Winner another insight into who God is. Because God is all-powerful, we can assume that redemption is "easy for God... a snap of the divine fingers." But Isaiah's image tells us how hard God is working to bring forth redemption. So, too, if I am partnering with God in the work of the new creation, then I also will experience times of pain, gasping, and panting.

Winner includes a prayer by St. Anselm of Canterbury, written in the eleventh century. Anselm employs another feminine image that Jesus himself gave us:

> *And you, Jesus, are you not also a mother?*
> *Are you not the mother who, like a hen,*
> *gathers her chickens under her wings?...*
> *It is by your death that [we] have been born...*

All images of God are incomplete. Words, sooner or later, fail us when we speak of Divinity. Yet, good images and metaphors can offer us deeper glimpses into who God is. And in doing so, they can enrich our relationship with the One who loves us far more than any words can say.

FOR REFLECTION

What do you feel and/or think about the image of God as laboring woman, as nursing mother?

Which images of God, especially images in the Bible, speak to you? Why do they speak to you?

Are there any images of God that do not speak to you? Why not?

YouTube Video 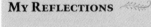 "Ave Maria," by Schubert, sung by Aida Garifullina

READERS' COMMENTS

"The image of God as a predominantly father figure has become off-putting for me. Not because of any animus against men, but because it feels so incomplete. One of my favorite Scripture quotes is from Psalm 131: 'Like a weaned child on its mother's lap, so is my soul within me.' I imagine God as that mother and I breathe and surrender myself into her tender arms."

"I worked for twenty-two years with women in labor, and there is no more touching image of God."

MY REFLECTIONS

 ## 34. Rocking Chair Prayer

In my retreat ministry, I travel all over the country. Frequently, I'm in airports. A few years ago, I began to notice something unusual in airports: rocking chairs! Not just one or two, but dozens of rockers all over the place. Many were white, others were a natural wood color, and some were even painted a rainbow of bright colors.

I've seen rocking chairs in airports in Philadelphia, Charlotte, Harrisburg, Boston, Miami, and Dallas. In fact, over a hundred airports all over the world now have rocking chairs. Why?

For one thing, airports are not conducive to rest and relaxation. They tend to be crowded and noisy places—with people and electric carts scurrying hither and yon. A rocking chair, as someone has said, can be "a pause button in a hectic environment." It's an island of peace amid a sea of bustle. Traveling these days can cause severe anxiety. But sitting for a few minutes in a rocking chair can help calm the most anxious traveler.

My retreat ministry also takes me to retreat centers all over the country. I've noticed that most of these places have rocking chairs too. I've seen rocking chairs in bedrooms, by fireplaces, in chapels, on porches, on decks, and on docks overlooking a pond or lake. People who operate retreat centers must know that rocking chairs are conducive to prayer and contemplation. It's easy to understand why this is so.

Many of us were probably rocked as infants. The gentle back and forth rhythm of the rocker imitated the rhythm we experienced in our mother's womb: the beating of her heart, the movements of her body, the pattern of her waking and sleeping. As infants, being held and rocked reassured us that we were not alone, that someone was taking care of us. Perhaps rocking in a rocking chair as an adult helps us to reconnect with this "blessed assurance."

When we rock in a rocker, our body is occupied. Our feet are making the rocker "go." This means we are less likely to fidget. At the same time, our minds are set free to explore, to ponder. When we rock back and forth, says poet Hilton L. Anderson, we are in touch with "The gentle flow of time / Measured in each rocking creak." She adds, we relax "in the metered now."

For some of us, the gentle back-and-forth motion of the rocking chair can become an invitation to talk with God. Here is a prayer I found myself saying as I rocked gently back and forth in a rocking chair.

A Rocking Chair Prayer

Back and forth... back and forth... back and forth I go...
While staying in one place, I am moving still...
    I am letting go.
In my rocking chair I am at one with the basic rhythms of life:
    back and forth... up and down... in and out... around and around.
I feel the thumping of my heart...
    I sense my breathing in and out...
And effortlessly I find myself praying:
O God of All Time, I am often anxious and worried about
    many things... calm me... calm me...
Reassure me I am not alone...
Let me feel your presence... your arms enfolding me...
Give me a deep sense of your care for me...
and remind me of your promises:
    "Everything's going to be okay."
Amid the rush of daily living, when I feel
    splintered into little pieces,
call me back to my rocking chair...
    where back and forth... back and forth...
I rest in your timeless love. Amen.

FOR REFLECTION

What has been your experience with rocking chairs?

Does anything stand out for you in this reflection?

YouTube Video
"Nada Te Turbe," by Taizé (from St. Teresa of Avila's prayer: "Let nothing disturb you")

"I'm reading this as I sit in a recliner that gently rocks. It's nice to start each day with the word of God and gentle rocking."

"I have the rocking chair that was my dad's. The wings on the back of the chair wrap around me and make me feel as if Dad's arms are embracing me."

MY REFLECTIONS

35. God Gives Matching Grants

You are probably familiar with the concept of matching grants. They work in many ways. If you contribute one hundred dollars to a non-profit like PBS, for example, another donor matches your donation. Or sometimes the grant organization will say to a non-profit's request: We will award you the grant to build that children's playground, but first you must raise twenty percent from other donors. Matching grants mean that no one—the requester, the donor, or the grant awarder—has to do all the work!

In her new book, *A Little Book of Light: Sparks of Hope, Moments of Prayer*, Alice Camille implies that God gives us matching grants. Before Jesus ascended into heaven, he gave his disciples a daunting task: "You will receive power when the holy Spirit comes upon you, and you will be my witnesses... to the ends of the earth" (Acts 1:8). Yikes! Sometimes it's hard to be a witness to Jesus in our own house!

But the key part of this evangelization mission is the *power of the Holy Spirit*. Camille writes, "If it were strictly up to you and me, Christianity would hardly make it down the block." She says that this vital role of the Spirit in our lives doesn't mean we get to stay in bed and let the Spirit do all the work. No: The Spirit lives in us. "It moves in concert with our efforts." I do my part (which might be ten percent or at times even only one percent), and the Spirit does the rest. Says Camille, "It's the best matching grant in the universe!"

Perhaps no story in the gospel illustrates "God's matching grant" better than the story of the multiplication of the loaves and fishes. In Mark's version, Jesus has just finished talking to a huge crowd— four thousand people. He is moved with pity for them because they are hungry. His disciples share his concern. They moan, "Where can anyone get enough bread in this deserted place to satisfy so many?" Jesus asks them, "What do you have?" They tell him they have five loaves and a few fish. Then Jesus tells the people to sit down. He takes the loaves and fish into his hands, offers thanks, and hands them to his disciples to distribute. The people eagerly eat and "are satisfied." There are even leftovers—seven baskets' worth!

This story doesn't merely describe something that happened over two thousand years ago—but something that continues to happen today. We do not have to do all the work to make our world a better place. We have only to give whatever we can—and the Spirit will do the rest. Sometimes the Spirit will act through others who join our efforts, and sometimes in other ways we can only marvel at.

I often see the Spirit acting in my talks and writing. Sometimes a listener will tell me they appreciated something I said, and I don't even remember saying it. Or I write an article, and someone tells me their favorite sentence, and that was the one I almost deleted.

Alice Camille concludes with another allusion to Scripture. She says, "Even though the yield of the soil to one hundredfold comes from God, the sower still has to get off the recliner and plant the seed. We do our little part, so the Spirit can multiply it."

FOR REFLECTION

Have you ever experienced the Holy Spirit "multiplying" something little that you gave?

What seed might you plant today?

YOUTUBE VIDEO   "Seed, Scattered and Sown," by Dan Feiten

READERS' COMMENTS

"As a teacher, I have former students say to me, 'Remember when you said...' And, in all honesty, I don't. To paraphrase [a quote often attributed to] Maya Angelou: 'Your students will not always remember what you taught them, but they will always remember how you made them feel.'"

"Our parishioners were helping a poor school in a village overseas. At our meeting, they asked me, 'What does the school need?' I said, 'A roof, floors, and student desks.' One man stood up and said he knew someone who would give us a matching grant. Our parishioners' generosity was the little boy's loaves and fishes."

MY REFLECTIONS

36. Hope and Worry

The other day, I was reflecting on some of the differences between hope and worry. Here's what I came up with.

Hope believes a better world is possible. Worry believes the world is getting worse.

Hope asks, "How can I help?" Worry asks, "What's the use?"

Hope trusts in God. Worry trusts in nothing.

Hope is afraid but takes the next first step. Worry is afraid to take any step—and just sits there.

Hope believes God is always with us. Worry thinks God has abandoned us.

Hope says, "I am only one, but I can do something." Worry says, "I am only one."

Hope engenders courage. Worry engenders timidity.

Hope energizes. Worry enervates.

Hope hangs on to Jesus' promises. Worry asks, "What promises?"

Hope is joyful. Worry is cynical.

Hope says, "Hang in there." Worry says, "Give up already."

Hope seeks out other hopeful companions. Worry is a loner.

Hope asks, "What can I do?" Worry worries.

Hope makes decisions. Worry worries.

Hope works hard. Worry worries.

Hope prays. Worry worries.

FOR REFLECTION

Do you agree or disagree with anything said about hope and worry in this reflection? If so, what and why?

Do you find yourself anywhere in this reflection?

Would you add anything to this reflection?

YouTube Video 〜 "Earth to God," by John Rich. In using this song, I am not implying that God is somehow out there in outer space and far removed from what's happening here on earth. On the contrary, I believe God is incarnate and active in our world—in creation, in humanity, and in our current world situation. But this song speaks to me because it humbly acknowledges our great need for God's grace right now to direct us and give us strength.

Readers' Comments 〜

"I had a fall several weeks ago and broke my right hand and damaged my right shoulder. I am in the process of recovery and doing intense physical therapy. I came home today from therapy feeling very worried and depressed about my recovery and future. I sat down and just read this reflection. My hope was renewed by the end. God knew I needed this today."

*"HOPE to me means **Hang On—Pain Ends!**"*

My Reflections 〜

37. Praying with Isaiah 49:8–15

There are many ways to pray with Scripture: reading the passage slowly and prayerfully, choosing a sentence and using it as a mantra throughout our day, or putting ourselves into the Scripture story we are reading. Another way is to dialogue with God about the Scripture reading. Here is my conversation with God using an excerpt from Isaiah 49. Isaiah's words are in bold print; mine are in italics.

Thus says the Lord: *Hold it right there, Lord. I see great power in these four little words. It's Isaiah's way of saying, "Listen up, people!" (I'm a people!) "The Lord has something important to say to you." That's why I'm praying with these words today, my Lord. I'm listening for something—anything—you might be saying to me today in this passage.*

In a time of favor: *Let me stop there again, God. Isn't every time a time of favor? My faith and my experience tell me there is no time when you cannot pour your love and grace down upon us... upon me. In good times and bad. When I have clarity of vision or when I'm inching my way through the fog. Anytime can be a time of your favor.*

In time of favor, I answer you. *I hate to quibble with you, my Beloved One, but I don't always hear you answering me. Or, if I'm more honest, your answer might not be the answer I want, so I close my ears. Or maybe your answer doesn't come in words, but in silence. And your silence demands humble waiting on my part. And, as you very well know, God, I am not always good at waiting. You can blame that on my Creator! (Hee-hee!)*

Say to the prisoners: Come out! *When I read these words, I see images of individuals being released from prison—especially those in prison for decades for crimes they did not commit! What joy on their faces... tears...*

hugs from family and friends. You, my dear Lord, are eager to free us from our "prisons"—those habits or attitudes that restrict our freedom as children of God.

To those in darkness: Show yourselves! *What are some of the darknesses I need to be released from, God? The darkness of fear... ignorance... pain... the feeling of abandonment... my past injuries... my personal shame... my hopelessness? Where do I start? Where do WE start, Loving Lord?*

Along the roadways they shall find pasture... They shall not hunger or thirst. *God, I thank you for the nourishment you have given me throughout my life: my family... your magnificent creation... your Scriptures and Mass... my education... all those individuals you put into my life who encourage me by the example of their faith and goodness. There is no end to the nourishment you provide for me, for us, along our earthly journey! Thank you, thank you!*

For he who pities them leads them and guides them. *God, you are my GPS! You point me in the right direction. And when I stray, please help me to recalibrate my steps that lead back to you.*

I will turn all my mountains into roadway, and make my highways level. *Beloved One, you're a civil engineer too! How crazy is that? You clear the way before me using Scripture, my daily prayer, and even my trusted friends.*

Can a mother forget her infant, be without tenderness for the child of her womb? *The answer to that question is (tragically) yes, she can. And men, too, can forget the children they have fathered. But that doesn't negate the countless men and women who have welcomed children into their lives and are doing the hard, hard 24/7 work of good parenting. I thank you, God, for all of them!*

Even should she forget, I will never forget you. *Really, God? Never? Even when I forget you? How precious are these words to me. They mean you can never un-remember us. You can never stop loving us, because that's who you are: Love. Eternal Love!*

FOR REFLECTION

Did any words or phrases stand out for you in this reflection?

How do *you* pray with Scripture?

YOUTUBE VIDEO
"I Will Never Forget You, My People," by Carey Landry, sung by the Sunday 7 p.m. Choir

READERS' COMMENTS
"These words stood out for me: 'Please free me from habits and attitudes that restrict my freedom as a child of God.' Thank you for sharing this insight. I have work to do."

"Isn't it amazing and mind boggling that no matter where we are, whatever we do or forget to do, God never leaves us?"

MY REFLECTIONS

38. Seeking God
in the "Land of Unlikeness"

The poet W.H. Auden has written a beautiful poem called "For the Time Being: A Christmas Oratorio." In it he suggests that we seek God in three unusual places. One of those places is the "Land of Unlikeness." He's saying, I believe, that we must seek God in people, places, and circumstances that are unlike ourselves, that is, in things that are different from us, unfamiliar to us, or even toward which we may feel a natural aversion.

When we look at our world today, we can be shocked or frightened by what is happening around us. We see wars; mass migrations of people fleeing violence and extreme poverty; natural disasters such as drought, fires, famine; mass shootings; political divisiveness; financial crises. Talk about the Land of Unlikeness! We may be tempted to retreat to a place more to our liking, a place that feels safer. Eventually, we may raise the burning question: "Where is God in all this bad news?" I think Auden's answer to that question would be this: *God is here*. God resides in the Land of Unlikeness: that is, in the confusion, anxiety, fear, and uncertainty.

Years ago, I came across the phrase "the tyranny of personal preference." That's powerful! It tells us our world becomes small if we surround ourselves only with people who are like us or to whom we are naturally drawn. Or if we shun every situation that makes us uncomfortable. If we do this, we miss out on a lot of personal growth and the opportunity to broaden our vision. More importantly, we miss finding God in places we never thought to look.

What would Jesus say about seeking God in the Land of Unlikeness? Wasn't the Incarnation itself a great venture into the Land of Unlikeness? The Divine becoming human? During his earthly life, Jesus often willingly entered the Land of Unlikeness.

He befriended men and women, wealthy and poor, healthy and sick, Jew and Gentile. From his parables we glean that Jesus hung out with farmers, shepherds, housewives, parents, children—many of these individuals unlike him in significant ways. His encounters with such people broadened his perspective. The feisty Syro-Phoenician woman, for example, even caused him to widen the scope of his mission.

Then there's Jesus greatest teaching: Love one another—even your enemies. We often become enemies when we fail to see any likeness between ourselves and "the other." In extreme cases, we can label some individuals "monsters," denying even our shared humanity with them.

Our news headlines sometimes thrust us into the Land of Unlikeness. But our faith tells us that even in this land, God is bestowing graces upon us. One of the most obvious graces is this: A renewed realization and appreciation that the earth is our common home... we are all interconnected... and we all share a common humanity. These truths are stronger and deeper than our unlikenesses.

Let us pray: Jesus, we ask for the grace to find you in the Land of Unlikeness. When love or duty calls us to greater selfless loving, help free us from "the tyranny of personal preference." May we welcome individuals into the circle of our lives who are unlike us in significant ways. Help us to be more open to personal growth and the broadening of our perspective. We ask for these graces through the power of your daring and persistent Holy Spirit. Amen.

FOR REFLECTION ✦

Have you ever "crossed over" into the Land of Unlikeness? What was that experience like for you?

What are your feelings and thoughts about our current news headlines? Does anything give you hope?

YOUTUBE VIDEO ✦ "Holy Spirit, Come and Fill This Place," sung by CeCe Winans, video by Lisa Deaton

READERS' COMMENTS ✦

"Even the imperfectly healed can be agents of healing. I hope I am listening with respectful attention to voices of outrage who clamor for justice. I hope I am unlearning 'the tyranny of personal preference.' The human capacity for love has not been made extinct by our nation's recent turmoil. And that, above all, gives me hope."

"I live where recently two dams broke in neighboring towns. These past two weeks I have watched humanity at its best. Total strangers giving food, shelter, and clothing to total strangers. A beautiful thing to witness."

MY REFLECTIONS ✦

39. Ordinary People Doing Good Things

We hear enough stories these days about people doing mean or bad things: bullying someone, stealing from the elderly, throwing garbage in a river, vandalizing a historic building. People doing bad things makes headlines. So, here are five true stories I've come across about ordinary people doing good things.

Food for Firefighters

Two firefighters were waiting in line to order at a fast-food place. Suddenly, the siren sounded in their truck. They went to leave when a couple who had just received their orders handed them their food. The firefighters accepted gratefully. The couple got back in line. When they placed their order, the manager declined to take their money.

My Mother's Flowers

When the clerk in the supermarket tallied my groceries, I was twelve dollars short. I began to remove some items from the bags, when another customer stopped me and held out a twenty dollar bill. I started to protest, but he said, "Please let me do this. My mother is in the hospital with cancer. Every day I visit her and bring her flowers. She insisted that I stop bringing the flowers and do something worthwhile with the money. So please accept this. It's my mother's flowers."

My Favorite Blanket

When I was seven, my family was driving to the Grand Canyon. As we drove along the highway, my favorite blanket suddenly flew out the car window and was gone. I was devastated. A little while later we stopped at the service plaza. My mother and I sat on a bench to eat our sandwiches. But I continued to mope. Suddenly a motorcycle gang pulled into the parking lot. One big man, complete with a dark beard and leather jacket, got off his bike and walked toward us. He asked us, "Is that your blue Ford?" My mother nodded nervously. From inside his jacket, the man pulled out my blanket and handed it to us. As he headed back to his bike, I ran after him and thanked him the only way I knew how: I gave him half my sandwich.

Young Hero on a Bicycle

One day I locked my car keys and phone in my car in the parking lot. Angrily, I kicked one of the tires and muttered a few choice words. A teenage boy on a bike saw me, stopped, and asked if something was wrong. I explained the situation. "I can't even call and ask my wife to bring me her car key, because this is our only car." The boy said, "Here, use my phone to call your wife and I'll get the key and bring it to you." I protested, "It's at least a seven-mile round trip." He insisted. About an hour later he returned with the key. I offered to pay him, but he declined, saying, "That's okay. I needed the exercise." And he rode away.

Special Needs Cats

Terry volunteers at the Safe Haven Pet Sanctuary, a no-kill cat sanctuary, in Green Bay, Wisconsin. Every day he comes in and brushes the special needs cats. Often, he falls asleep. Safe Haven wrote an appreciation post on Facebook for Terry. Immediately, people started donating money to the sanctuary in Terry's honor. The donations soon exceeded ten thousand dollars. Safe Haven said, "We are lucky to have a human like Terry."

And we are lucky to have ordinary people like these doing good things!

For Reflection

Do any of these stories speak to you today?

Have you ever witnessed an ordinary person doing a good thing?

Have you ever been that ordinary person who helped someone in need?

YouTube Video   "Kindness," by Steven Curtis Chapman

Readers' Comments

"What heart-warming stories. Each act of kindness brought tears to my eyes, especially the story about the flowers."

"On a Wisconsin winter day (windchill 40 below) I was driving to the store when I saw an elderly man in a motorized wheelchair moving into a lane of traffic. I pulled my car to the side of the road, ran over to him, and asked if I could help him. He said he had lost his mittens in the road, and he really needed them. I told him I'd get them for him if he moved off the road to safety. When I returned the mittens, he asked me my name. I felt such a presence of God at that moment. What a blessing!"

My Reflections

40. Acceptance Speech for the Gift of Life

Whenever I watch awards shows, I am intrigued by the acceptance speeches. That's when the recipients thank the people who made winning the award possible: family, co-workers, "my Lord and Savior." I thought, I should write a thank-you speech to God for being awarded the gift of life. Here's the speech I imagine giving right before I emerged from my mother's womb...

Acceptance Speech for the Gift of Life

I wish to thank our Creator God for this precious gift of life.
I am truly honored to be the recipient of so great a gift.
I never expected to receive this gift of a
   single, unique human life.
I never asked for this gift. I also assure you that I have
   done nothing to merit this priceless treasure.
So, I come before you amazed... humbled...
   and extremely grateful.
Speaking of gratitude, I would like to thank my
   parents in a special way for cooperating with our
   Creator to share their own gift of life with me.
Mom, Dad, I wouldn't be here today if it weren't for both of you.
Since I have been entrusted with the gift of life,
I would like to make a few promises to God.
First, I promise never to take my life for granted. Never.
Second, I will respect the lives of my fellow
   recipients of this same precious gift:
Those who have gone before me.
Those who walk this earth alongside me.
And those who will come after me.

Third, I will never use this gift in any way
that betrays the love with which it was entrusted to me.
Instead, I will endeavor to use my life as a
    lifelong investment in loving,
in whatever form or length of time my loving may take.
And fourth, if I fall short of these promises
    (and I already sense I will),
I will seek our Creator God's forgiveness,
for I know the Giver of all gifts is rich in mercy
    and overflowing with loving-kindness.
I now sense my birth is imminent.
I am about to wiggle from my mother's
    warm and life-sustaining womb
and venture out into the big and beautiful world awaiting me.
I sense there are people with my mother
    helping to deliver me safely.
One is even waiting to catch me in their open hands.
As I take my first breath, Beloved Creator God, know this:
My birth cry is my way of saying Thank you! Thank you!
I pray that these same words will be on my lips
    when I take my last earthly breath too.

FOR REFLECTION

Who has helped you to see that your life is a precious gift
from God?

What are some ways we make our lives "a lifelong investment
in loving"?

YOUTUBE VIDEO   "Wild and Precious Life," by JJ Heller

READERS' COMMENTS

"I was very moved by your speech and the song by JJ Heller. I have a heart filled with gratitude for the four extraordinary children my husband and I were gifted with! And now two amazing grandchildren! God is so generous!"

"Thank you for reminding us how precious LIFE is. I forwarded your speech to a Pregnancy Center that supports preborn babies and their mothers and fathers."

MY REFLECTIONS